The
Microwave
Italian
Cookbook

The Microwave Italian Cookbook

Thelma Snyder
and
Marcia Cone

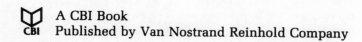

A CBI Book
Published by Van Nostrand Reinhold Company

Copyright (c) 1984 by Thelma Snyder and Marcia Cone

Library of Congress Catalog Card Number 83-14450

ISBN 0-442-28060-2

Printed in the United States of America

Designed by Laura Bernay

Photographs by David Arky

Published by Van Nostrand Reinhold Company, Inc.
135 West 50th Street
New York, New York 10020

Van Nostrand Reinhold Company Limited
Molly Millars Lane
Wokingham, Berkshire RG11 2PY, England

Van Nostrand Reinhold
480 La Trobe Street
Melbourne, Victoria 3000, Australia

Macmillan of Canada
Division of Gage Publishing Limited
164 Commander Boulevard
Agincourt, Ontario M1S 3C7, Canada

16 15 14 13 12 11 10 9 8 7 6 5 4 3 2 1

Library of Congress Cataloging in Publication Data

Snyder, Thelma.
The microwave Italian cookbook.

Includes index.
1. Microwave cookery. 2. Cookery, Italian. I. Cone, Marcia. II. Title.
TX832.S556 1984   641.5'882   83-14450
ISBN 0-442-28060-2

Microwave ovens cook food differently than standard ovens. In order to prepare the recipes in this book safely and successfully, follow precisely the directions given.

Contents

Acknowledgments

Thanks to friends and family
who were so supportive during the months that it took
to make the sauce-stained manuscript
into a finished book.

To Charles F. Lamalle, importers,
1123 Broadway, New York, for dishes;

to Todaro Brothers,
557 Second Avenue, New York 10016, for food and dishes;

to the Italian Wine Center,
499 Park Avenue, New York 10022;

to Kress' Liquor Store,
1 Berlin Road, Cherry Hill, New Jersey 08034;

to David Arky, for the photographs.

Introduction

"There is no love sincerer than the love of food," said Bernard Shaw. He would certainly approve, then, of a country that locks its shops for three and a half hours at lunchtime; closes schools and government offices at 2:00 P.M., and shuts ski lifts for an hour at noon . . . all for the love of food.

In Italy, this phenomenon is called *mezzogiorno* (pronounced mezo-joorno), which literally means midday. But *mezzogiorno* is recognized by all as a hallowed institution. It is the biggest meal of the day and a time when people go home to have a glass of wine, relax, and share the good things of life. The concept is contrary to everything we have learned from our puritan work ethic, but if we can get beyond that initial resistance, we can come to appreciate Italy as a country whose people prize food as much as mother and the church. Any nation that is so devoted to food must have something to teach us about cooking and dining.

With that thought in mind, we began to ask ourselves, how can we adapt Italian cooking to a nation of clock watchers? A three-and-a-half-hour lunch on a regular basis is out of the question. But with *The Microwave Italian Cookbook* in hand, it is possible to prepare those Italian specialties *presto* in the microwave oven.

By way of background, what we Americans know as Italian cooking has been much influenced by the first waves of Italian immigrants who came to this country from southern Italy. It is just in the last ten years that we have become acquainted with the differences between northern and southern cooking, and even more recently have we realized that

1

there are regions within regions that follow different cooking styles.

As we traveled through Italy, perusing bookstalls for authentic cookbooks, we noticed that many books began with a map of Italy that was divided into those regions. A brief look at Italian history reveals that the country was not united until about 100 years ago. Before that time, Italy was a collection of city states each with its own government, culture, and cooking.

Some regional generalities are that spaghetti and olive oil are predominant in the south, while the north boasts of rice and butter. Bread is made with salt in the south, but the salt content gradually decreases as one moves north to the salt-free bread of Tuscany. Regional kitchens are so diverse that children study them in school.

Our recipes are representative of all parts of Italy. From northern Valle d'Aosta comes Fonduta, a close relative of Swiss fondue. Fettuccine alla Carbonara is a product of Rome, and the purest Salsa di Pomodoro, tomato sauce, comes from Calabria in the south.

Something that all Italian cooking has in common is that it relies on the best fresh ingredients, and this is one reason it varies from region to region. That is also why the best dishes do not require added expense for ingredients, but a little common sense. Pears are best in the winter, so that is the time to prepare Pere allo Zabaione e Cioccolato. Fresh Italian plum tomatoes are found in early fall, and fresh basil for Pesto in the summer.

Italians are as loyal to the specific order in which their foods should be eaten as they are to freshness. One usually begins with an *antipasto*, or appetizer. This is followed by a *primo*, or first course, of pasta or soup. Then a *secondo*, or second course, which is the meat, fish, or chicken; the *contorno* is the vegetable, which may accompany or follow the *secondo*. The *insalata* or salad follows the *secondo*. The final course is a piece of fresh fruit or cheese, and for special occasions a *dolce* or sweet dessert.

If you are wondering whether a scorecard or libretto would be helpful to keep track of what course is coming next, we found that practice will make you familiar with the order. What is more evident is that in the Italian home a skilled *nonna* (grandmother) is key to the preparation of such an elaborate feast. Before you decide that the delights of Italian cooking are too complicated and lost to you forever, glance through the recipes and cooking times in this book.

We have taken recipes from Italy and our favorite Italian restaurants in the United States and adapted them to the microwave to save you half to three quarters of the time. Sauces are completed in a flash and need little stirring. In most cases the microwave pasta sauces can be finished in the time that it takes to boil the water and cook the pasta on a conventional stove. This is a case of complementary cooking between microwave oven and conventional stove.

Beyond pasta sauces, zucchini and eggplant become tender in the microwave without losing their shape, and shorter cooking times allow each to retain its fresh flavor and vitamin value. With the clay simmerpot, veal shanks are heated to produce a fork-tender Ossobucco; the clay retains more cooking juices to be later thickened into a sauce. Ossobucco is traditionally served with Polenta, a cornmeal dish, or Risotta alla Milanese, a creamy rice dish flavored with saffron. Both side dishes take less time and less trouble in the microwave and produce better results than would be achieved on the conventional stove. This is because minimal stirring is required and more moisture is retained during cooking.

Pizza is a natural for microwave cooking, because the yeast dough can be both raised and cooked in the microwave. When made into small rounds, this pizza recipe becomes an alluring appetizer or late night snack.

Italian ice cream, which any Italian will tell you is the best in the world, can now be part of your world. The milk and egg base, a requirement for good Italian ice cream, is cooked in the microwave and then frozen in an ice cream maker or by freezer trays.

From *antipasti* to *dolci*, *The Microwave Italian Cookbook* will add a new dimension to your everyday cooking and encourage your zest for more fanciful entertaining. And *that* is what the Italians would call *la dolce vita*.

1

Guide for Successful
Italian Cooking:

Microwave Techniques,
Menu Planning, Utensils,
and Ingredients

TERMS USED IN RECIPES: *Arranging foods* with the thicker sections toward the outside permits more even cooking. This is because the majority of microwave energy is received by the foods on the outer edges of the dish.

Cooking powers designated in the recipes will be one of these four, which are based on a standard 600- to 700-watt oven.

High	(100%)
Reheat	(80%)
Medium	(50%)
Low	(10%)

Foods that benefit from lower power settings are those with more delicate ingredients such as sauces, and those incorporating eggs or cheese. Less tender cuts of meat also need lower power settings to lengthen cooking time for tenderization and development of flavors.

Once the power is listed in the recipe it remains the same throughout the recipe, unless otherwise stated. Powers will be italicized if we feel the power change to a lower one might be overlooked.

Cooking time is the time it takes to cook the recipe. If no cooking is involved, a preparation time to assemble ingredients is given.

Cover with lid or vented plastic wrap means to cover with a dish lid or, when no lid is available, plastic wrap that is folded back slightly on one corner to allow some heat and steam to escape. Covering in this manner keeps the food moist and shortens the cooking time.

Cover, loosely, with wax paper means to lay a piece of wax paper on top of the dish to prevent spatters and speed cooking in foods which do not need steaming to tenderize.

Cover with paper towel to absorb excess moisture while allowing steam to escape, as when cooking fish.

If *no cover* is mentioned, the food is cooked uncovered.

Cover with foil to protect larger bone areas from overcooking as in the recipe calling for leg of lamb. Wrap foil smoothly and tightly as directed so that no rough edges protrude. Foil can be used on the ends of large meats also, if they appear to be cooking too quickly.

Doubling of recipes is possible. Use the same procedure and power setting of the original recipe, but rather than doubling the cooking time, add half again as much time to equal 1½ times that in the original recipe.

Rearranging dishes placed in a circular pattern in the oven means to switch positions according to how the food is cooking.

Repositioning food within the dish ensures continued even cooking.

Rotating or turning a dish clockwise is used sometimes with foods which can't be stirred, repositioned, or turned over. Rotating will mean either one half, one third, or one quarter turn depending on the frequency of rotation called for in the recipe. It is quite possible that your oven's cooking pattern is even enough that dishes require little or no rotation.

Serving sizes of most of the recipes have been designed for 4 to 6 persons. In the Italian way, meals can be expanded to serve more by adding another course and serving smaller portions of each. Doubling recipes is also possible; see above.

Standing time allows foods to finish cooking by heat conduction. (Heat is built up by the rapid movement of food molecules during cooking.) Unless otherwise stated, foods should stand on a flat surface, rather than a cooling rack, to allow the internal heat to work within the food. Denser foods, like meats, will stand for 10 minutes. During this time the internal temperature will rise 10° to 15°F. Less dense foods, like fish or vegetables, will stand less. In this case, standing time may not be mentioned if it seems no more than the time necessary to go from kitchen to table.

Turning over is necessary, partway through cooking, for recipes that call for large pieces of meat like leg of lamb or a roast.

MENU PLANNING: *For everyday eating*, when there are time constraints, you will probably choose one main-course meat, or a pasta, to be served along with a salad and bread. Plan the meal around the cooking time of the main dish. If a vegetable is desired, cook it during the standing time of that dish. Most vegetables will take no more than 10 minutes to cook, which will fit into this time slot.

Italian-style eating is a leisurely process, most likely reserved for the weekend or when company comes. To eat in this manner, the *antipasti* would be followed with a *primo* or first course of pasta or soup, then a *secondo* of meat or fish. The vegetable, *contorno*, could be served with the main dish. An *insalata*, salad, would follow, and finally, fresh fruit, cheese, or a *dolce*, sweet, would be served.

Antipasti and desserts are often best when they are made earlier in the day, for sake of convenience and because the flavors often improve with time. In most cases the *antipasti* blossoms into full flavor when served at room temperature. So if you have refrigerated them, allow time in the microwave or on the kitchen counter to take the chill off. When using the microwave, cover the refrigerated dish (unless the food is breaded and would become soggy), and heat on Medium (50% power) for 1 to 2 minutes.

Soups can be prepared earlier in the day and will become more savory as the day goes on. Reheat the entire amount or prepare individual servings, as desired. A time-consuming pasta, such as Lasagne, can be prepared right before serving, or prepared earlier in the week and reheated (see recipe for timing).

● *Order of Preparation*: Now the question comes, "When do I cook a *secondo*, or main-dish course, so that it is timed to follow the *primo* smoothly; or what goes into the oven when?" Here are some answers:

● Choose a quick and light *secondo*, like chicken cutlets or fish. Do all preparations for the *secondo*, short of cooking, and pop it into the oven between courses. A *secondo* like this is good when following a course like Lasagne.

● Start the longer-cooking main dish, interrupt to cook the *primo* pasta sauce, and resume cooking the main dish while eating the pasta. The stew won't be ruined, and in fact will take less time to finish cooking once it has had a chance to equalize temperatures.

● During the standing time of the main dish, prepare the vegetable.

● For specific menu suggestions, see Suggested Menus for Entertaining (p.145).

UTENSILS: *Browning dishes* have been treated with a special material that absorbs microwave energy. When preheated in the microwave, the center area rises in temperature to between 200° and 600°F. This enables foods to be seared and browned, while being cooked for short periods of time.

Browning dishes come in varying sizes and are in either the grill type—a flat dish with a well to catch juices—or a casserole with sides and a lid.

A *casserole* is a round or oval dish at least 3 inches deep which may come with its own lid. When a food is being brought to a boil, the casserole should be twice as deep as the food inside to avoid the possibility of overcooking. An oval casserole is perfect for microwave cooking because it has no corners where microwave energy builds up to overcook foods.

A *3-quart casserole* with a lid will be invaluable when it comes to making sauces and soups. It is as important as your large pasta pot for conventional cooking. The lid makes stirring and re-covering so much easier. If you have no lid, or it breaks, we find an inverted microwaveproof plate is a good substitute.

A *custard cup* is a glass or ceramic vessel holding about 6 ounces in volume.

A *flat dish*, with dimensions given, is called for when foods need to be arranged in one layer to cook evenly and quickly. Pie or cake plates can be used here if they are large enough to hold the volume of food.

A *food processor* or blender can save preparation time in recipes calling for chopping, grinding, or mixing.

A *microwave dish* means a glass or ceramic dish that transfers microwave energy to the food. It should not have any silver trim and should be able to withstand heat up to 400°F.

One- and four-cup glass measures are called for often. We find them handy utensils to use for measuring, cooking, and pouring.

Ramekins are small porcelain or glass casseroles holding about 6 ounces in volume.

A *roasting rack* is a utensil of ceramic, tempered plastic, or paper, that enables meat to be raised above the dish in which it cooks. This prevents overcooking of the underside of the meat or steaming of foods where a drier crust is desired.

A *3-quart simmerpot* is a porous clay pot with lid that is soaked in cold water, overnight before the first usage, and for 15 minutes before each subsequent use. The bottom is glazed and the lid is unglazed. The purpose of the clay pot in conventional and microwave cooking is to aid in tenderization of tough meat cuts. We find that the clay simmerpot improves flavor and texture of any dish where it is used. It is worth investing in!

INGREDIENTS: Good recipes deserve high-quality, fresh ingredients for the best results. Here are some specific ingredients we find critical to success. If you have trouble finding them in your area, check the Acknowledgments.

Amaretti cookies are dry, almond-flavored Italian cookies.

Beans, or legumes, called for in this book, are either Great Northern or kidney beans, which most closely approximate the white beans found in Italy.

Beef stock or chicken stock should be made according to the recipe given, or purchased.

Butter that is unsalted is preferred over salted or a margarine substitute.

Bread crumbs should be unseasoned, preferably made from Italian bread in your food processor or blender.

Capers are the buds of a wild plant preserved in wine vinegar.

Cheese: There are a few types that need to be mentioned here. *Parmesan* is familiar to most of us, but if possible it should always be freshly grated at the store, or in your home. You will marvel at the difference between the freshly grated as compared to the prepackaged. The best type is Parmigiano-Reggiano. Italian *Fontina* cheese is preferred to the Danish for flavor and texture upon melting.

If cheese is to be served with fruit or bread sticks, it is most flavorful at room temperature. Bring 1/2 pound refrigerated cheese to room temperature by heating on Medium (50% power) for 45 seconds to 1 minute, depending on the density of the cheese.

Herbs should be fresh whenever available. Basil, in particular, when called for in pesto, certain pasta sauces, and antipasto salads must be fresh. We have given dry alternatives where applicable. When you have an abundance of herbs, chop them and freeze them in moistureproof containers for later use.

Lemon juice should be fresh because it is far superior to the bottled product. To get more juice from your lemons, place 1 or 2 lemons in the microwave on Low (10% power) for 1 minute.

Olive oil varies in quality from brand to brand. Generalizations are: Imported is better than domestic, the greener oil or the one labeled *extra virgine* is better. An exception is that we have found some California olive oils to be very good and less expensive than imported. We feel that the *extra virgine* is only necessary for uncooked appetizers and salad dressings. For cooking, a good flavored oil will be fine.

Once opened, olive oil should be kept in containers with lids having holes to allow air circulation. Divide large cans of oil into jars and store in the refrigerator for longer life. The oil will become cloudy and solidify upon refrigeration, but this can be remedied by bringing it to room temperature in the microwave. Remove the jar cap and heat on Medium (50% power) for 1 to 5 minutes, depending on amount, just until it turns clear.

Pancetta is a rolled cut of bacon that is salt-cured and unsmoked. Many books will call for blanched bacon in its place. We feel that an acceptable substitute is bacon (without blanching), prosciutto, or boiled ham.

Parsley, depending on availability, should be wide-leafed Italian parsley, which is more flavorful than curly parsley.

Pasta will either be fresh (purchased or homemade), or dry boxed pasta. Fresh pasta takes less time to cook and should be cooked until tender, for the *al dente* doneness is almost impossible to achieve with fresh pasta. Dry pasta (*pasta secca*), on the other hand, can be cooked to *al dente*, or with a bite. The best boxed pastas are made of pure semolina.

Rind of lemon or orange should include the outer colored part only, not the bitter white portion underneath.

Pignoli are the small, beige nuts we call pine nuts. They are often found in Mediterranean and Middle Eastern cooking.

Prosciutto is cured unsmoked ham.

Radicchio is a leafy vegetable that looks like a red and white cabbage but is similar to lettuce.

Rice (Arborio) is grown in the northern Italian Po River Valley. It is a short-grain rice with a white spot in the center, and it can be found in specialty or Italian grocery stores. In some areas, you will be able to find a "pearl rice" which is close to the Arborio. If you have no luck in finding that, use long-grain rice. It won't have quite the same texture, but will cook in the same time and be perfectly acceptable.

Saffron is dried, red stigma of the crocus, which turns whatever it is cooked with to a daffodil yellow. It is expensive but, fortunately, only a small amount is needed for the Risotto alla Milanese.

Semolina is yellow, fine-textured durum wheat which is an ingredient found in the best brands of pasta. We prefer it for pasta and pizza doughs because of the superb texture, color, and flavor it produces, although ordinary wheat flour is an acceptable substitute. Semolina can be purchased in Italian or specialty stores, and should not be mistaken for farina which is very similar in appearance.

Sausage should be sweet Italian sausage or a blend of sweet and hot sausages, according to taste.

Tomatoes peel easily when plunged into boiling water. Pour enough water into a microwave casserole to cover the number of tomatoes to be peeled. Cover the water with a lid or vented plastic wrap, to speed boiling, and heat the water on High until it comes to a boil. Remove the bowl from the oven, and plunge each tomato into the water for a few seconds. Remove tomatoes and peel.

Canned tomatoes should be Italian plum tomatoes, preferably those from the San Marzano region.

White truffles are highly esteemed for their flavor in cooking and are peculiar to the Piedmont region of Italy. Their appearance belies their value in cooking. When you find them in specialty stores, be prepared to pay a bundle for these inauspicious gray, stonelike lumps (they are actually a fungus).

2
Antipasti

Appetizers

We came to know and love *antipasti* on one of those brilliant October days in Calabria that Italians take for granted. An Italian friend of ours decided to take us for a drive. It turned out to be an exhilarating ride as we careened over mountain roads from Nicastro, at the top of the Italian instep on the Tyrrhenian Sea to Reggio di Calabria, the tip of the boot. Our goal was to see *i bronzi de Riace*, the two Greek bronze statues cast around 450 B.C., which had recently been salvaged from the ocean floor, stirring curiosity and arousing unexpected affection from Italians. Even with the importance of the mission, our guide designed the trip so that we would be finished admiring the *bronzi* in time for *mezzogiorno*, or midday meal.

As we walked to the entrance of the restaurant we could gaze across the aquamarine Straits of Messina to the island of Sicily. Ferry boats ruled the seas now, but it was not hard to imagine the days when Ulysses might have navigated his Greek vessel along this course.

As we entered the glass-enclosed restaurant by the sea, we were guided past the most enticing *antipasto* table we had ever seen. Deep red tomatoes and eggplant turned ebony from roasting shimmered like gems under oil. Rows of stuffed mushrooms and peppers stood at attention beside a regal-looking leg of Parma ham. These in turn were flanked by an aromatic pastel seafood salad and a polenta the color of goldenrod, stuffed with hard-cooked eggs and ham. As we think back, the overwhelming sense of history surrounding our journey blends with fond memories of food. The result is the certainty that *antipasti* should always be an exciting introduction to dining pleasure.

The recipes in this chapter are designed to be the course before pasta or soup, for *antipasto* means "before the pasta." Each can be served alone, or three or four can be combined in a buffet-style appetizer table.

For instance, platters of Peperoni Arrosti e Funghi all'Olio (Roasted Pepper and Mushroom Salad), Insalata di Riso (Rice Salad) served in red-pepper cups, and Gamberetti all'Olio e Limone (Shrimps Marinated in Oil or Lemon) make a nice marinated salad selection. To complete the collection, add Caprino Marinati con Rosmarino (Goat's Milk Cheese Marinated with Rosemary), fresh tomato slices and Italian bread or slender bread sticks. Allow each dish to come to room temperature before serving to bring out the full flavor.

For a hot *antipasto* table we suggest Pomodori Ripieni (Stuffed Tomatoes), Cappelle di Funghi Ripieni (Stuffed Mushroom Caps), and Vongole Ripieni (Stuffed Clams).

Caponata
COLD EGGPLANT APPETIZER

Quantity: 4 cups   **Cooking time: 12 minutes plus 1 to 2 hours to chill**

½ cup olive oil
1 garlic clove, minced
2 onions, sliced thin
2 celery ribs, sliced thin
2 medium-size eggplants, peeled and diced
1 medium-size tomato, peeled and chopped

¼ cup capers, drained
2 tablespoons pignoli (pine nuts)
2 tablespoons red-wine vinegar
1 teaspoon dried orégano, crushed
½ teaspoon salt
¼ teaspoon freshly ground pepper

In a 2-quart microwave casserole with lid, combine oil, garlic, and onions. Cover and cook on High for 2 minutes or until onions are slightly tender, stirring once. Add celery, cover, and cook for 2 to 3 minutes more, or until celery is slightly tender, stirring once. Add eggplants, cover, and cook for 6 to 8 minutes more, or until eggplants are tender, stirring once. Stir in remaining ingredients.

Cover and chill for 1 to 2 hours to develop flavors; stir occasionally. Can be stored in the refrigerator for up to 2 weeks, but is best served at room temperature.

Bagna Cauda
ANCHOVY DIP

Bagna Cauda means "hot bath"; the bath is a unique blend of ingredients used as a dip for bread cubes or raw vegetables. Italian villagers in Piedmont would make this in an earthenware pot. If you have one, be sure to test the pot first to determine if it is microwave safe.*

Servings: 6 to 8   Cooking time: 3 minutes

2 ounces flat anchovy fillets,   *4 ounces unsalted butter*
   minced   *4 garlic cloves, minced*
½ cup olive oil   *¼ teaspoon salt (optional)*

Place anchovies in a 1- or 2-quart earthenware pot and mash with a fork. Add remaining ingredients and cook on High for 1½ to 2 minutes, until butter is melted and begins to foam, stirring once. Mix thoroughly to make a smooth sauce.

Bagna Cauda can be kept warm over a flame, while dipping vegetables, or can be returned to the microwave on High for 30 seconds.

Suggested vegetables for dipping:
Celery hearts
Broccoli flowerets or peeled
   carrots, cut into ½-inch slices
Radishes or zucchini, cut into ½-
   inch slices
Spinach, young crisp leaves
Peppers, cut into long thin slices

VARIATION   To use Bagna Cauda as a dressing, cut garlic cloves into thin slices instead of mincing them. Cook according to basic recipe. Spoon mixture over 4 roasted peppers (the garlic pieces will give a deliciously nutty flavor). Serve with crusty bread to sop up the excess sauce. Serves 4 as a first course.

TIP   You may wish to give each person his or her own ramekin filled with warm sauce.

*Test an earthenware pot by placing it on the bottom shelf of the microwave oven beside 1 cup cold tap water in a glass measure. Microwave on High for 1 minute. If the pot remains relatively cool and the water begins to heat, the pot is not absorbing any microwave energy and will be fine for cooking. If the pot gets hot, don't use it for microwave cooking.

Fonduta
CHEESE FONDUE WITH TRUFFLES

This dish is from the mountainous regions of Valle d'Aosta and northern Piedmont that border Switzerland. The consistency of the melted mixture is somewhat thinner than the more familiar Swiss fondue, but the buttery Fontina cheese of Valle d'Aosta adds an incomparable richness to fonduta. The white truffles are native to Piedmont. However, since truffles are a trifle too costly for most of us, you may eliminate them without sacrificing much of the original flavor.

Quantity: 3 to 4 cups   **Cooking time: 10 minutes**

1 teaspoon cornstarch
1 cup light cream
1 pound Italian Fontina cheese,
  diced
3 egg yolks, beaten
¼ teaspoon freshly ground white
  pepper

Pinch of salt
1 or 2 small white truffles, fresh
  or canned, sliced thin
  (optional)
Cubes of Italian bread

Place cornstarch in a 1½-quart microwave casserole, suitable for serving. Stir in ½ cup cream until cornstarch is dissolved. Add diced cheese and cook on Medium (50% power) for 4 to 7 minutes, until cheese has almost melted but is not completely smooth, stirring once or twice.

Meanwhile, in a separate bowl, lightly beat egg yolks, pepper, and salt with a wire whisk. Beat in remaining ½ cup cream. Slowly stir egg-cream mixture into melted cheese. Cook on Medium for 2 to 3 minutes, or until mixture is smooth and creamy, stirring once or twice. Sprinkle with truffles, if desired.

Serve in the cooking dish, or divide among individual ramekins. Surround with bread cubes, spearing with forks to dip into cheese.

TIPS   Although Italian Fontina has superior flavor, it may not always be readily available. When necessary, substitute Gruyère or Danish Fontina, or a mixture of ¾ pound mozzarella and ¼ pound Bel Paese.

Medium power heats the cheese slowly to prevent a rubbery texture.

Verduri Marinati
MARINATED VEGETABLES

This colorful platter of tender-crisp vegetables in wine marinade is a refreshing stimulant before the meal.

Servings: 8 as first course

Cooking time: 10 minutes plus 4 hours to chill

Marinade:
3 tablespoons olive oil
1 garlic clove, minced
1 large sprig of Italian parsley
¼ cup dry white wine
2 tablespoons lemon juice
1 tablespoon wine vinegar
1 bay leaf, crushed
1 sprig of fresh orégano, or ¼ teaspoon crushed dried
½ teaspoon salt
¼ teaspoon freshly ground black pepper

6 ounces small mushrooms, or large mushrooms halved
6 ounces zucchini (2 small), washed but not peeled, cut lengthwise into very thin slices
6 ounces green snap beans, ends removed and halved
6 ounces carrots, peeled and cut into thin 2-inch sticks

Combine marinade ingredients in 2-quart microwave casserole. Cook on High for 2 minutes, stirring halfway through cooking.

Slide mushrooms into warm marinade and cook on High for 1 to 1½ minutes until just tender, stirring halfway through cooking. Remove mushrooms with a slotted spoon and arrange on a large serving platter.

Slide zucchini slices into marinade and cook for 1 to 1½ minutes until tender-crisp, stirring halfway through cooking. Transfer with a slotted spoon to serving platter.

Slide green beans into marinade and cover with lid or vented plastic wrap. Cook for 2 to 3 minutes until tender-crisp, stirring halfway through cooking. Transfer with slotted spoon to serving platter with other vegetables.

Slide carrots into marinade and cover with lid or vented plastic wrap. Cook for 2 to 3 minutes until tender-crisp, stirring once halfway through cooking. Arrange carrots on platter.

Pour remaining marinade over vegetables. Cover and refrigerate for 4 hours or overnight. Remove garlic clove after 4 hours.

Serve at room temperature as a first course or salad course.

TIP   Covering green beans and carrots is necessary to ensure that these dense vegetables cook completely.

Peperoni Arrosti e Funghi all'Olio
ROASTED PEPPER AND MUSHROOM SALAD

Servings: 4

Cooking time: 10 minutes plus 2 to 3
hours to marinate

2 red sweet peppers
2 green sweet peppers
1 medium-size Spanish onion,
    cut into ¼-inch slices
¼ pound mushrooms, cut into
    thin slices
2 tablespoons pignoli (pine nuts),
    optional

¼ cup olive oil
2 tablespoons lemon juice
½ teaspoon dried orégano,
    crushed
½ teaspoon salt
¼ teaspoon freshly ground
    pepper

Roast peppers as described in Peperoni Arrosti (see Index), or char under the broiler. Cut into ½-inch strips.

Place onion in a 1-quart microwave casserole. Cover with lid or vented plastic wrap and cook on High for 1 minute, until slightly tender.

Add roasted pepper strips to cooked onion. Stir in mushrooms and pignoli.

In a 1-cup glass measure, combine oil, lemon juice, orégano, salt, and pepper; pour over vegetables and mix well. Allow to stand at room temperature for 2 to 3 hours for flavors to develop. Serve at room temperature.

TIP   Salad can be stored, covered, in refrigerator for up to 2 days.

Pomodori con Prosciutto e Basilico
TOMATOES WITH PROSCIUTTO AND BASIL

It is best to make this recipe when basil is in season. The fresh flavor is hard to imitate with dried basil, and fresh basil leaves in the center of the plate make an attractive presentation.

Servings: 4   **Cooking time: 5 minutes**

1 pound red ripe tomatoes,
  preferably plum, cut into ¼-
  inch slices
1 teaspoon olive oil
Freshly ground pepper

2 ounces thin-sliced prosciutto
4 ounces mozzarella cheese
1 tablespoon finely chopped fresh
  basil, or ½ teaspoon crushed
  dried

Arrange tomatoes in 1 overlapping, circular layer on the outside rim of a 10-inch round microwave dish. Sprinkle with olive oil and pepper to taste.

Cut prosciutto into pieces. Slice cheese to fit the size of tomato slices. Insert prosciutto and cheese slices between tomato slices. Sprinkle with basil.

Cover loosely with wax paper and cook on Medium (50% power) for 2 to 5 minutes, or until cheese melts.

TIP   Wax paper is used to retain steam so the cheese melts more evenly.

Cappelle di Funghi Impannato
BREADED MUSHROOM CAPS

Mushrooms, when deep fried, are often overwhelmed by batter and oil. The light Parmesan and bread-crumb mixture called for here helps to enhance the mushrooms' delicate flavor. Serve them as a tasty garnish with any meat dish.

Servings: 4 to 6   **Cooking time: 2 minutes**

12 ounces fresh mushrooms
¼ cup olive oil
1 teaspoon minced garlic
¼ cup fine dry bread crumbs

2 tablespoons grated Parmesan
  cheese
1 tablespoon finely chopped
  parsley

Remove stems from mushrooms and reserve for use in soups or salads. Wipe mushroom caps clean and set aside.

In a small glass bowl or 1-cup glass measure, combine oil and garlic. Cook on High for 1 minute until garlic is tender but not brown.

Meanwhile, in a plastic bag, combine remaining ingredients and shake well to mix.

Dip 3 or 4 mushrooms into garlic-oil and then into crumb mixture, shaking bag to coat mushrooms. Place coated mushrooms, cap side up, on a microwave roasting rack and continue the process until all mushrooms are coated. Cook on High for 1½ to 2 minutes, until caps are heated through but still firm.

TIP   The microwave rack elevates the mushrooms from direct contact with the dish to eliminate steaming.

Cappelle di Funghi Ripieni
STUFFED MUSHROOM CAPS

These mushroom caps serve as the vehicles for a béchamel sauce sparked with Parmesan and prosciutto. They are heavenly, but rich.

Servings: 6   Cooking time: 12 minutes

12 fresh mushrooms, each approximately 2 inches in diameter, or 24 smaller mushrooms
4 tablespoons butter
1 tablespoon finely chopped onion
4 tablespoons flour
1 cup milk
¼ teaspoon salt

⅛ teaspoon white pepper
¼ cup chopped thin-sliced prosciutto or cooked ham
2 tablespoons finely chopped parsley
3 tablespoons grated Parmesan cheese
2 tablespoons fine dry bread crumbs

Remove stems from mushrooms and reserve for use in soups or salads. Wipe mushroom caps clean, and arrange cap side down in circular rows on the outside of a round microwave serving dish.

In a 4-cup glass measure or bowl, combine butter and onion. Cook on High for 1 to 2 minutes, or until onion is slightly tender. Stir in flour to blend. Slowly pour in milk, beating constantly. Cook on High for 5 to 7 minutes, until sauce is boiling and thickened, beating 2 or 3 times. Stir in salt and pepper. Stir in prosciutto, parsley, and cheese.

Divide the sauce evenly among the mushroom caps. Sprinkle bread crumbs over all. Cook on High for 2 or 3 minutes, until filling is heated through, rotating twice.

TIP   Stuffed mushrooms may be prepared and refrigerated for final cooking later. If they have been refrigerated, cook on High for 2 to 5 minutes.

Pomodori Ripieni
STUFFED TOMATOES

Servings: 4   Cooking time: 8 minutes

4 large ripe tomatoes
2 tablespoons oilve oil
½ cup finely chopped onion
¾ cup fine dry bread crumbs
¼ cup pignoli (pine nuts)

¼ cup grated Parmesan cheese
2 tablespoons chopped parsley
1 tablespoon lemon juice
1 tablespoon capers (optional)
Salt and pepper

Slice tomatoes ½ inch from the top, and discard tops. Scoop out cores and seeds. Place tomatoes, hollow side up, in a 9-inch round microwave baking dish.

In a medium-size glass or microwaveproof mixing bowl, combine oil and onion. Cook on High for 1 to 2 minutes until onion is slightly tender, stirring once. Stir in remaining ingredients, adding salt and pepper to taste; mix well. Spoon filling into tomato cavities.

Cover tomatoes with wax paper and cook on High for 3 to 6 minutes, until tomatoes and filling are heated, rotating 2 to 3 times. Allow to stand for 1 minute before serving.

TIP   Wax paper is used to speed up cooking but, unlike a lid or plastic wrap, it won't cause the tomatoes to become watery.

Carciofi Ripieni
STUFFED ARTICHOKES

We tasted a dish similar to this in Naples, an area where artichokes and tomatoes are plentiful and savored.

Servings: 4   Cooking time: 20 minutes without sauce
                                              preparation time

4 medium-size artichokes
½ cup olive oil
2 teaspoons minced garlic
1 cup fine dry bread crumbs
¼ cup freshly chopped parsley
¼ cup grated Parmesan cheese
1 teaspoon chopped fresh
  orégano, or ¼ teaspoon
  crushed dried

¼ teaspoon salt
⅛ teaspoon freshly ground
  pepper
2 cups Salsa di Pomodoro I,
  Tomato Sauce I (see Index), or
  prepared tomato sauce

Cook artichokes as described in Carciofi (see Index).

After artichokes have cooled, gently press leaves away from the center and spoon out inner choke with a small spoon or melon baller.

In a medium-size bowl, combine olive oil and garlic. Cook on High for 1 minute, until garlic is tender but not brown. Stir in bread crumbs, parsley, cheese, orégano, salt, and pepper; mix well. Set aside.

Spoon 1 cup of the tomato sauce into a 2-quart microwave casserole. Place artichokes, bottom down, in the casserole with the sauce. Spoon the stuffing into the center cavity of the artichokes and in between the outer leaves with a teaspoon. (See photograph.) Pour remaining 1 cup tomato sauce over the artichokes.

Cover with lid or vented plastic wrap and cook on High for 4 to 8 minutes, until sauce is bubbling and stuffing is heated through, rotating dish 2 or 3 times. Allow to stand, covered, for 2 minutes before serving.

To serve: Place each artichoke in a shallow bowl and spoon some of the sauce over top. Use sauce for dipping leaves.

TIP   The moisture from the sauce and the tight cover allow the artichokes to cook quickly and evenly.

Insalata di Riso
RICE SALAD

Your tendency might be to cook this rice until it is fluffy and dry. But resist the temptation! The consistency of cooked Arborio rice (short-grain Italian rice) should be moist and still firm to the bite.

Mound the salad in sweet red pepper halves for a lovely first course or luncheon dish.

Quantity: About 3 cups

Cooking time: 14 minutes plus 1 hour to chill

1¾ cups water
1 cup Italian Arborio or short-grain rice, or Converted long-grain rice
¼ cup pitted and thinly sliced black olives
¼ cup chopped Peperoni Arrosti, Roasted Peppers (See Index), or pimiento
2 tablespoons drained capers, or pignoli (pine nuts)
¼ cup chopped fresh parsley
¼ cup sliced scallion

Dressing:
1 tablespoon wine vinegar
1 teaspoon lemon juice
½ teaspoon Dijon mustard
½ teaspoon salt
¼ teaspoon freshly ground pepper
¼ cup olive oil

Lettuce leaves or sweet peppers for serving

Pour water into a 3-quart microwave casserole. Cover with lid or vented plastic wrap and cook on High for 4 to 6 minutes, or until water boils. Add rice and stir. Re-cover and cook on *Medium* (50% power) for 6 to 8 minutes, until rice swells but remains firm to the bite. Do not stir. Allow to stand, covered, for 10 minutes.

Add olives, chopped pepper, capers, parsley, and scallion to rice.

In a small bowl, combine dressing ingredients, stirring to blend. Pour over rice; stir. Chill for 1 hour.

Serve at room temperature in lettuce cups or seeded sweet pepper halves.

VARIATIONS   Substitute ½ cup Maionese, Mayonnaise (see Index) and 1 teaspoon Dijon mustard for dressing ingredients.

For Insalata di Riso con Pollo, Rice Salad with Chicken, add 1 cup cubed cooked chicken with the olives.

TIPS   Hot water can be more readily absorbed by the rice in cooking. Stirring while rice is cooking will cause it to break up and become starchy.

Torta di Zucchini
ZUCCHINI TART

This *torta* is something like a pizza but with a delicate butter pastry crust. Topped with colorful concentric circles of zucchini, or with tomato as a variation, it serves as an attractive appetizer or picnic lunch.

Servings: 6   Cooking time: 15 minutes plus 1 hour
                                                      to chill dough

1 cup flour
⅜ teaspoon salt
5 tablespoons butter, cut into 20
  cubes
1 egg, slightly beaten
3 small zucchini, about 10
  ounces altogether, cut
  crosswise into ⅛-inch slices

4 ounces mozzarella cheese,
  grated
Freshly ground pepper
1 tablespoon chopped fresh basil,
  or ½ teaspoon crushed dried
1 tablespoon olive oil

In a large mixing bowl or on a countertop, combine flour and ⅛ teaspoon salt; mix well. Add butter with fingertips, pastry blender or 2 knives; working quickly, cut butter into flour until particles are pea-size.

Stir in egg with a fork, and form dough into a ball. Do not overwork or dough will become tough. Flatten ball into a pancake approximately 4 inches in diameter; this will make it easier to roll out dough later. Cover with plastic wrap and refrigerate for 1 hour or up to 3 days.

On a 15-inch square of wax paper, lightly floured, roll pastry into a circle slightly larger than 10 inches in diameter. Trim edges with a pastry cutter or sharp knife to form a neat 10-inch circle.

Cut another 15-inch square of wax paper and place under pastry and paper to make a double layer of wax paper. Prick top surface of pastry with a fork every ½ inch or so, and place on bottom shelf of oven. Cook on High for 4 to 6 minutes, or until dry, opaque, and cooked through (pastry will not brown), rotating every 2 minutes. With a wide spatula, gently slide pastry from paper to a cooling rack. Allow to cool for 5 to 10 minutes, then transfer to a flat serving platter.

Place zucchini in a 1-quart microwave casserole. Cover with lid or vented plstic wrap and cook on High for 2 to 4 minutes, or until tender-crisp, stirring once. Allow to stand for 1 minute.

Sprinkle all but 1 tablespoon grated cheese on the pastry crust, leaving a ½-inch border along the edge. Arrange zucchini slices in overlapping circular layers on top of the cheese. Sprinkle with re-maining ¼ teaspoon salt, pepper to taste, basil, and olive oil. Place remaining 1 tablespoon cheese on top of the zucchini. Cook on *Medium* (50% power) for 3 to 6 minutes, or until cheese is melted, rotating 2 to 3 times. Serve hot or at room temperature.

Wine Selection: Gavi

VARIATION   Replace zucchini with 2 medium-size ripe tomatoes. Do not precook tomatoes, but cut into ⅛-inch slices and arrange on pastry crust sprinkled with cheese in the same manner as zucchini. Cook tart according to basic recipe.

TIP   When making dough in a food processor, after egg is added, process only until dough forms small granules; then remove from bowl and form a ball with your hands. Overprocessing will make dough tough.

Bruschetta
TOASTED GARLIC BREAD

A specialty of Tuscany and Umbria, Bruschetta is traditionally heated over burning embers to be enjoyed by all as a prelude to the meal.

Quantity: 10 to 12 slices   **Cooking time: 4 minutes**

¼ cup olive oil
1 teaspoon minced garlic
4 ounces mozzarella cheese, grated
1 tablespoon lemon juice
1 tablespoon finely chopped fresh parsley

⅛ teaspoon freshly grated pepper
1 ounce anchovies, drained and minced (optional)
½ loaf of Italian bread, cut into ½-inch slices

In a custard cup, combine oil and garlic. Cook on High for 30 seconds to 1 minute.

In a small bowl combine remaining ingredients except bread.

Place a large microwave browning dish in oven and preheat according to manufacturer's instructions for toasted sandwiches, about 3 to 5 minutes on High.

Meanwhile, brush both sides of bread with garlic oil. On one side of each bread slice, place 1 tablespoon of cheese mixture and press down lightly. Place bread, cheese side up, onto hot browning dish. Cook on High for 2 to 3 minutes, or until cheese melts, rotating dish after 1 minute. Serve hot.

Cozze alla Marinara
MUSSELS IN WINE BROTH

You'll want a loaf of crusty Italian bread on hand to soak up every last drop of tantalizing broth.

Servings: 4   **Cooking time: 8 minutes**

2 tablespoons olive oil
2 garlic cloves, minced
¼ cup dry white wine

¼ teaspoon hot pepper flakes
¼ cup chopped fresh parsley
2 dozen large mussels, cleaned

In a 3-quart microwave casserole with lid, combine oil and garlic. Cook on High for 45 seconds. Add wine, pepper flakes, and parsley. Cook on High for 1 to 2 minutes, or until liquid boils. Add mussels and cover. Cook on High for 3 to 5 minutes, or until all mussels are opened, stirring halfway through. Allow to stand for 2 minutes.

Discard any unopened mussels. Serve in soup bowls with the broth and Italian bread.

TIP   The care of mussels: Place in cold water as soon as you bring them home (if necessary, cover the bowl and keep refrigerated until the next day). Discard any broken or even slightly opened shells. Remove any hard beard with a knife, then scrub shells and wash them in several clean batches of cold water. The water should appear clean in final rinsing.

Cozze al Maionese con Acciuga e Capperi
MUSSELS WITH ANCHOVY CAPER MAYONNAISE

Servings: 6 to 8   Cooking time: 8 minutes plus 1
                                               hour to chill

1 medium-size onion, chopped   3 pounds mussels, cleaned
1 garlic clove, crushed   1 cup Maionese con Acciuga
½ cup dry white wine   Capperi; Mayonnaise with
3 parsley sprigs   Anchovies and Capers (see
1 bay leaf, crushed   Index)
4 peppercorns, crushed

In a 4-quart microwave casserole with lid, combine all ingredients except mussels and mayonnaise. Cover and cook on High for 3 to 4 minutes. Add mussels. Re-cover and cook on High for 3 to 4 minutes more, or until all mussels are opened, stirring once.

Discard any unopened mussels and chill in the liquid, covered, for 1 hour.

To serve: Remove mussels from liquid and arrange on a serving platter. Top each mussel with some of the mayonnaise.

Wine Selection: Greco di Tufo

Gamberetti all'Olio e Limone
SHRIMPS MARINATED IN OIL AND LEMON

Servings: 8

Cooking time: 5 minutes plus 1 to 1½ hours to marinate

1 pound small shrimps (if medium shrimps, cut into halves)
¼ cup olive oil
3 tablespoons lemon juice
1 tablespoon wine vinegar

¼ teaspoon freshly ground pepper
Lettuce leaves
3 tablespoons chopped Italian parsley for garnish

Arrange shrimps in a single layer in a 9-inch-round microwave dish. Cover with vented plastic wrap and cook on High for 2 minutes; reposition shrimps from the outside to the inside, and vice versa. Recover and cook for 1 to 3 minutes more, or until all shrimps have turned opaque and bright pink in color; do not overcook. Allow to cool slightly and remove shells.

Meanwhile, in a medium-size bowl, combine olive oil, lemon juice, vinegar, and pepper. Add cooked shrimps to this mixture and allow to marinate at room temperature for 1 to 1½ hours, stirring occasionally. Serve at room temperature on lettuce leaves with parsley garnish.
Wine Selection: Orvieto

TIP   Shrimps can be refrigerated in marinade overnight, then reheated to bring to room temperature on Defrost (30% power) for 1 to 3 minutes.

Vongole Ripieni
STUFFED CLAMS

Servings: 4 to 6   **Cooking time: 10 minutes**

2 dozen Little Neck clams
2 tablespoons olive oil
1 garlic clove, minced
2 tablespoons finely chopped
  parsley
½ cup fine dry bread crumbs

2 tablespoons freshly grated
  Parmesan cheese
1 teaspoon fresh orégano, or ¼
  teaspoon crushed dried
Lemon wedges for garnish

Open clams and detach clams from shells. Position each clam on half of the shell and discard the other half. Place clams on shells around the outer edge of a 12-inch round or oval microwave serving dish or tray.

Meanwhile, in a small glass or microwaveproof bowl, combine oil and garlic. Cook on High for 45 seconds until garlic is tender but not brown. Stir in remaining ingredients except lemon wedges and mix well.

Spoon about 1 teaspoon garlic-bread mixture on top of each clam. Cook on *Medium* (50% power) for 8 to 10 minutes, until clams are cooked through, rotating twice during cooking. Allow to stand for 2 minutes before serving. Serve with lemon wedges.

Wine Selection: Corvo Bianco

TIP   Medium power is used to cook clams to prevent "popping," or the quick build-up of steam under the clam membrane which causes it to burst.

Caprino Marinati con Rosmarino
GOAT'S MILK CHEESE MARINATED WITH ROSEMARY

Servings: 4 to 6   Preparation time: 5 minutes plus
                                                    1 hour to chill

This is not a microwave recipe, but we found the marinated cylindrical cheese so simple to prepare and so complementary to the other recipes that we included it as a selection for an *antipasto* table.

¼ *pound Caprino or mild goat's*   2 *tablespoons extra virgin olive*
  milk cheese   *oil*
1 *heaping teaspoon fresh*
  rosemary

Roll cheese in rosemary to coat. Place cheese in a small serving dish and pour oil over it. Marinate at room temperature for 1 hour.
Serve with crackers.
Wine Selection: Nebbiolo d'Alba

VARIATION   If Caprino is not available, a cow's milk cheese called Caprini Mauri is an acceptable substitute.

3
Minestre

Soups

In an Italian meal, the soup course follows the *antipasti* and is a replacement for the pasta course. "*Mama mia*," you say, "nothing can replace pasta!"

We must confess that even in Italy we often talked ourselves out of the soup course in anticipation of the pasta. We knew that we could always count on pasta to impart a satisfaction we believed to be unequaled by any other food. But ignorance is often bliss. We now find that Italian soups have the ability to comfort like a soothing bath on a winter day or *mama mia's* generous hug.

To clear up some of the mystery surrounding Italian soups, a *minestra* is any soup containing a starch such as pasta, rice, or potatoes. A *minestrone* is a thick vegetable soup, a *brodo* is a broth, and a *zuppa* is any clear or thickened broth with additional ingredients. In this country, an Italian soup is versatile enough to commence a meal or can become the main dish with only salad or bread for accompaniment.

If you are unsure of where to begin the exploration of Italian soups, here are a few suggestions. Pasta e Fagioli, with pasta predominant, is not surprisingly one of our favorites, but it is filling and should be followed by a light meat course or salad. By contrast, Minestra del Paradiso, chicken broth with bread crumb puffs, is a light and fragrant soup.

Minestrone alla Genovese with pesto sauce is unrivaled when it comes to flavor complexity, and seems to make a better midday meal than first course. For a satisfying supper dish try Zuppa di Frutta di Mare, a fish and shellfish soup with a dash of red pepper.

The Italian beef and chicken stocks that follow will be the bases for all the other soups in this chapter and are distinguished from French stocks by the addition of tomato. Use your imagination to expand their usage, and add leftover rice or noodles to them. Unadorned *pasta in brodo* is a perfectly respectable way to begin the midday or evening meal.

Brodo di Manzo
BEEF STOCK

Quantity: about 4 cups   **Cooking time: 1¼ hours**

3 pounds meat bones, cracked,
   with scraps and marrow
4 cups water
2 medium-size onions, quartered
1 tomato, quartered
1 carrot, sliced

1 celery rib with leaves, sliced
¼ cup chopped fresh parsley
1 bay leaf, crushed
2 whole cloves
1 teaspoon salt
4 whole peppercorns

Combine all ingredients in a 4-quart microwave casserole or simmerpot
with lid. Cover and cook on High for 15 minutes, stirring occasionally.
Re-cover and cook on *Medium* (50% power) for 60 minutes. Allow to
stand, covered, for 5 minutes. Strain.

Brodo di Pollo
CHICKEN STOCK

Quantity: about 5 cups   **Cooking time: 1½ hours**

3 pounds chicken backs, necks,
   and wings, or a 3-pound
   chicken, cut up
4 cups water
1 celery rib with leaves, sliced
1 medium-size carrot, sliced
1 onion, quartered

1 tomato, quartered
¼ cup chopped fresh parsley
2 whole cloves
1 bay leaf, crushed
1 teaspoon salt
4 whole peppercorns

Combine all ingredients in a 4-quart microwave casserole or simmerpot
with lid. Cover and cook on High for 15 minutes; stir. Re-cover and
cook on *Medium* (50% power) for 75 to 80 minutes, stirring occasionally.
Allow to stand, covered, for 5 minutes. Strain.

TIP   Use remaining chicken in recipes calling for cooked chicken
such as Insalata di Riso con Pollo, Rice Salad with Chicken (see Index).

Minestra del Paradiso

SOUP OF PARADISE

This is a simple chicken broth topped with a mixture of beaten eggs and bread crumbs; our version of one originally fashioned by the nineteenth-century gourmand, Pellegrino Artusi. The egg mixture is light and airy, and resembles clouds when spooned onto the hot broth. Can there be any better description of this soup than *paradiso*?

Servings: 4   **Cooking time: 8 minutes**

2 cups chicken stock
2 eggs, separated
2 tablespoons fine dry bread
   crumbs
1 tablespoon grated Parmesan
   cheese

⅛ teaspoon freshly grated
   nutmeg
Fresh parsley, snipped as garnish

Pour stock into a 4-cup glass measure. Cover with vented plastic wrap and cook on High for 4 to 6 minutes, or until boiling.

Meanwhile, in a small bowl beat egg whites until they form soft peaks. In a separate bowl beat yolks until frothy. Stir bread crumbs, Parmesan, and nutmeg into yolks. Fold in egg whites.

Divide stock into 4 microwaveproof bowls. Spoon one quarter of the egg mixture onto each bowl of soup, dropping it lightly on top of the broth; egg mixture will float.

Place bowls in oven and cook on High for 2 minutes, or until egg mixture is set, rotating and repositioning halfway through cooking.

Garnish each bowl with sprinkling of nutmeg and some snipped parsley.

Zuppa di Scarola e Polpettine
ESCAROLE AND MEATBALL SOUP

Escarole is a variety of curly-leaved endive, more commonly used for cooking in Europe than in this country. In this recipe escarole adds a nice texture counterpoint to the meatballs in broth.

Servings: 6   **Cooking time: 17 minutes**

1 head of escarole, about 1 pound
2 tablespoons butter
6 tablespoons finely chopped onion, about 1 medium-size
½ pound lean ground beef or veal
1 egg, beaten
1 tablespoon finely chopped parsley

1 tablespoon grated Parmesan cheese, plus more to serve with soup
2 tablespoons fine dry bread crumbs
¼ teaspoon salt
Pinch of freshly ground pepper
Pinch of freshly grated nutmeg
4 cups chicken or beef stock
6 thin slices of lemon as garnish

Wash escarole well; dry. Remove base and white portion of leaves and cut remaining green leaves into ¼-inch strips.

In a 3-quart microwave casserole with lid, combine butter and 3 tablespoons onion. Cover and cook on High for 1½ minutes, until onion is slightly tender. Add escarole, cover, and cook on High for 4 to 6 minutes, or until tender, stirring once.

Meanwhile, in a medium-size bowl, combine remaining 3 table-spoons onion, the beef or veal, egg, parsley, 1 tablespoon grated cheese, bread crumbs, salt, pepper, and nutmeg. Stir to mix, and form into 1-inch meatballs.

Add meatballs and stock to escarole. Re-cover and cook on High for 8 to 10 minutes until boiling, stirring twice; soup will become frothy and slightly thickened in the last 2 minutes of cooking. Allow to stand, covered, for 5 minutes before serving.

To serve: Ladle into soup bowls and sprinkle with cheese. Garnish with lemon slices.

Minestrone alla Genovese

MINESTRONE IN THE GENOAN STYLE

The Genoans claim to have invented minestrone. While this may or may not be true, they certainly do lay claim to a delicious version, more like a vegetable stew than a soup. The basil sauce (Pesto), stirred in at the table, is not an option but instead makes this the best vegetable soup you will ever taste.

Servings: 6 to 8   **Cooking time: 40 minutes**

2 tablespoons olive oil
1 tablespoon butter
1 garlic clove, minced
1 medium-sized onion, sliced
  thin
1 cup peeled and diced potato
  (1 large)
½ cup thin-sliced celery (1 rib)
½ cup peeled and thin-sliced
  carrots (1 medium)
½ cup sliced zucchini (1 small)
1 cup ½-inch pieces of green
  snap beans (about ¼ pound)
1½ cups shredded cabbage
  (about ½ small head)
3 cups beef or chicken stock

1 cup peeled and seeded ripe
  tomatoes, preferably plum, or
  undrained canned, chopped
2 tablespoons finely chopped
  parsley
1 teaspoon finely chopped fresh
  basil, or ¼ teaspoon crushed
  dried
Freshly ground pepper
1 cup cooked Great Northern
  beans (as in Fagioli, see Index)
  or canned cannellini beans
¼ cup small dry pasta
Freshly grated Parmesan cheese
Pesto (see Index)

In a 4-quart microwave casserole with lid combine oil, butter, garlic, and onion. Cover and cook on High for 2 to 3 minutes, stirring once until vegetables are slightly tender. Stir in potato, celery, and carrots. Cover and cook for 2 to 4 minutes more, stirring once.

Stir in zucchini, green beans, and cabbage. Re-cover and cook for 2 to 3 minutes, stirring once.

Add stock, tomatoes, parsley, and basil; stir. Cover and cook on High for 10 to 12 minutes, until soup boils, stirring once. Turn power down to *Medium* (50% power) and cook for 15 to 20 minutes until potato is almost tender, stirring occasionally. Add pepper to taste.

Add beans and pasta; stir. Cover and cook on Medium for 8 to 12 minutes, until pasta is almost tender. Allow to stand, covered, for 5 minutes before serving.

Ladle soup into bowls and sprinkle with cheese and a spoonful of pesto.

Risi e Bisi
RICE AND PEA SOUP

A sprightly green and white soup which is a Venetian specialty of the spring. Because of the seasonality of the dish it is best to use fresh sweet peas for optimum flavor and texture.

Servings: 6   **Cooking time: 20 minutes**

2 tablespoons butter
1 medium-size onion, chopped
2 pounds fresh peas, or 1
* package (10 ounces) frozen*
* peas, about 1½ cups*
4 cups chicken stock
1 cup short-grain rice, preferably
* Arborio, or Converted long-*
* grain*

3 tablespoons finely chopped
* parsley*
¼ teaspoon freshly ground
* pepper*
Salt
Freshly grated Parmesan cheese

In a 3-quart microwave casserole with lid, combine butter and onion. Cover and cook on High for 2 minutes until onion is slightly tender, stirring after 1 minute. Stir in fresh or frozen peas, re-cover, and cook for 2 minutes more; stir.

Stir in remaining ingredients, except cheese, with salt to taste. Cover and cook on High for 16 to 18 minutes, only until rice is still firm to the bite, stirring once.

Allow to stand, covered, for 5 minutes; rice will continue to cook during that time.

Serve with grated cheese.

TIP   If frozen peas are being used in place of fresh, do not defrost them but add while still frozen.

Zuppa di Lenticchie e Salsiccie
LENTIL AND SAUSAGE SOUP

Servings: 6 to 8   Cooking time: 1½ hours

½ pound Salsiccie con Semi di
   Finocchi, Sweet Sausage (see
   Index), or packaged sausage
1 medium-size onion, chopped
1 medium-size carrot, chopped
1 celery rib, chopped
2 tablespoons chopped parsley
1 cup peeled and chopped ripe
   tomatoes, preferably plum, or
   undrained canned, chopped
3 cups beef stock

1 cup dry red wine
2 cups dried lentils, soaked
   overnight or cooked following
   directions for Fagioli (see
   Index)
½ teaspoon salt
¼ teaspoon freshly ground
   pepper
Freshly grated Parmesan cheese
1 tablespoon grated carrot as
   garnish

Remove sausage casing and break up sausage.

In a 4-quart microwave casserole with lid, combine onion, carrot, and celery. Spread sausage on top of vegetables. Cover and cook on High for 5 to 7 minutes, until sausage loses pink color, stirring to break up sausage halfway through cooking.

Add remaining ingredients except cheese and grated carrot. Cover and cook on High for 15 minutes, stirring once. Re-cover and cook on Medium (50% power) for 70 to 80 minutes, or until lentils are tender and flavor is well developed, stirring occasionally. Allow to stand, covered, for 5 minutes.

Serve each bowl sprinkled with some freshly grated Parmesan cheese and grated carrot.

Minestra di Patate e Carote
POTATO AND CARROT SOUP

Servings: 6 to 8   Cooking time: 25 minutes

3 tablespoons butter
2 medium-size onions, chopped
  fine
1½ pounds potatoes, peeled and
  cut into ¼-inch slices
2 tablespoons water
1 cup milk
2 cups beef stock

2 medium-size carrots, peeled
  and grated
¼ teaspoon freshly ground
  pepper
Salt
3 tablespoons chopped fresh
  parsley
Freshly grated Parmesan cheese

In a 3-quart microwave casserole with lid, combine butter and onions. Cover and cook on High for 3 minutes until onions are slightly tender; stir. Add potatoes and water. Cover and cook on High for 10 to 12 minutes, until potatoes are tender, stirring halfway through cooking.

Force potatoes through a ricer or mash in the casserole. Return to casserole and pour in milk and stock, stirring constantly to make a smooth mixture. Add carrots, pepper, and salt to taste. Cover and cook for 8 to 10 minutes, until boiling, stirring once halfway through cooking. Allow to stand, covered, for 5 minutes before serving.

Top each bowl with some chopped parsley and pass the freshly grated cheese.

Pasta e Fagioli
PASTA AND BEAN SOUP

Hearty only begins to describe Pasta e Fagioli, the pasta-bean soup served at room temperature in the summer and hot for chillier days. We like to make this soup when we have a ham bone with a little meat, but you may substitute prosciutto or cooked ham.

Servings: 6   **Cooking time: about 1 hour**

3 tablespoons olive oil
1 garlic clove, minced
1 medium-size onion, chopped
  fine
1 medium-size carrot, chopped
  fine
1 celery rib, chopped fine
1 cup peeled and chopped ripe
  tomatoes, preferably plum, or
  undrained canned, chopped
3 cups beef stock
1 cup dried white kidney or
  Great Northern beans, soaked
  overnight, or cooked following
  directions for Fagioli (see
  Index), or 2 cups canned
  cannellini beans

1 ham bone with meat attached,
  or 2 ounces smoked ham or
  lean bacon, cut into 2-inch
  cubes
1 tablespoon finely chopped
  parsley
1/8 teaspoon dried hot pepper
  flakes
1/8 teaspoon freshly ground black
  pepper
3/4 cup small macaroni (ditali,
  tubetti, or elbows)
Salt
Freshly grated Parmesan cheese

Soak a 3-quart clay simmerpot in cold water for 15 minutes. Combine oil, garlic, onion, carrot, and celery in the simmerpot. Cover and cook on High for 2 minutes until vegetables are slightly tender, stirring once.

Add tomatoes, beef stock, beans, ham bone, parsley, hot pepper flakes, and freshly ground black pepper. Cover and cook on High for 10 minutes; stir. Cover and cook on *Medium* (50% power) for 35 to 45 minutes, or until beans are tender, stirring occasionally.

Add pasta and salt to taste. Cover and cook on *High* for 5 minutes to bring soup back to temperature; stir. Re-cover and cook on *Medium* for 3 to 5 minutes, or until pasta is cooked but still firm to the bite. Remove ham bone and allow to stand, covered, for 10 minutes; the pasta will continue cooking during this time.

Serve with freshly grated cheese.

TIP   A simmerpot produces a better result than a glass casserole.

Zuppa di Frutta di Mare
FISH AND SHELLFISH SOUP

Because of the accessibility of the sea, every region of Italy has some type of fish soup. This one is a colorful combination of pink shrimps, flaky white fish, and glistening black mussels. Red pepper gives it a spicy nip. As fish prices fluctuate throughout the year, feel free to improvise. Exclude shrimps when too expensive or substitute clams for mussels when available.

Servings: 6   Cooking time: 25 minutes

¼ cup olive oil
2 garlic cloves, minced
1 onion, chopped fine
1½ cups peeled and chopped ripe tomatoes, preferably plum, or canned undrained, chopped
2 teaspoons chopped fresh basil, or ½ teaspoon crushed dried
1 bay leaf, crushed
1 tablespoon finely chopped parsley
¼ teaspoon freshly ground black pepper
⅛ teaspoon dried red pepper flakes

¼ cup dry white wine
1 cup clam juice or water
1 pound squid, dressed and rinsed well, cut into ¼-inch circles, including tentacles; or substitute ½ pound fish fillets
2 pounds assorted lean fish fillets, cut into 1½-inch pieces (whiting, halibut, monkfish, freshwater or sea bass, or flounder)
1 dozen mussels, scrubbed clean
½ pound shrimps

In a 3-quart microwave casserole with lid, combine oil, garlic, and onion. Cover and cook on High for 2 minutes until vegetables are slightly tender. Add tomatoes, basil, bay leaf, parsley, black pepper, and red pepper flakes. Cover and cook for 4 minutes; stir.

Add wine and clam juice, cover, and cook for 2 to 6 minutes, or until mixture boils.

Add squid, re-cover, and cook for 2 minutes; stir. Add fish pieces, re-cover, and cook for 6 to 8 minutes, or until fish flakes, rearranging fish pieces halfway through cooking. Add mussels and arrange shrimps around the outside of the casserole. Cover and cook for 2 to 4 minutes, or until mussels are opened and shrimps turn pink. Allow to stand for 3 minutes, covered, before serving. Serve with garlic bread.

TIPS   Ask to have the squid dressed at your market, or prepare it yourself by first removing the 2 layers of skin, an outer speckled skin and a transparent skin underneath it. Remove the beak, eyes, what appears to be a plastic cartilage or backbone, and the inner digestive tract. Rinse well and dry. The cut circles of squid should be small, but if you have purchased a larger squid, cut these circles into halves to make pieces of convenient size.

If substituting ½ pound fish for squid, eliminate separate cooking step for squid and cook all fish together until they flake.

Zuppa di Cozze/Zuppa di Vongole
MUSSEL SOUP OR CLAM SOUP

This soup is chock-full of shellfish, with just enough broth for dunking. It is an irresistible first course for 4, or main course for 2.

Servings: 4   Cooking time: 12 to 15 minutes

¼ cup olive oil
2 garlic cloves, minced
1 cup peeled and chopped ripe
  tomatoes, preferably plum, or
  undrained canned, chopped.
1 tablespoon chopped fresh basil,
  or ½ teaspoon crushed dried

2 tablespoons finely chopped
  parsley
⅛ teaspoon red pepper flakes
2 pounds mussels or clams,
  scrubbed clean
Toasted Italian bread slices for
  dunking

In a 3-quart microwave casserole with lid, combine oil and garlic. Cover and cook on High for 1 minute until garlic is tender but not brown. Add tomatoes, basil, parsley, and pepper flakes. Cover and cook for 3 minutes more; stir.

Add mussels or clams, re-cover, and cook on High for 5 to 9 minutes, or until mussels or clams have opened, stirring once after 3 minutes. Allow to stand, covered, for 3 minutes. Discard any unopened mussels or clams.

Serve in soup bowls with broth and toasted bread for dunking.

TIP   Clams will take a little longer to cook than mussels and this is the reason for the time range.

4
Salse
Sauces

It might be said that sauces are the fulcrum upon which a cuisine pivots. In our opinion the Italian cuisine is no exception.

It is in this chapter that you will find the basic sauces which are the foundations for dozens of innovative dishes throughout the book. The obvious is tomato sauce, which is more than just a covering for spaghetti. A tomato sauce is often incorporated into meat dishes, or cooked with vegetables. We offer three to select from, depending on the ultimate intention for using the sauce.

Contrary to popular belief, simmering a tomato sauce all day doesn't necessarily add anything other than a fragrant perfume to fill the kitchen. (And granted, that is worth something.) But lengthy simmering on the conventional stove may make a sauce overly bitter. To achieve a full-flavored tomato sauce, we found it best to cook the sauce uncovered, for 30 minutes or less in the microwave. The result is a sauce that dares to be compared to *nonna's*.*

In addition to the meatless tomato sauces, you will discover two that do include meat. Ragu alla Bolognese, a rich meat sauce sweetened with red wine and carrot, and Ragu alla Casalinga, Home-Style Meat Sauce. The latter is less complicated and relies on canned tomatoes rather than fresh when time is of the essence and only kitchen staples are handy. But the tomato is not the last word when it comes to Italian sauces.

---

*Italian for "grandma's"; it is the grandmothers of Italy who cook the tomato sauces.

Let us call attention to the white sauce or Salsa Balsamella used in lasagne. In its various forms it can complement macaroni, spaghetti, and *antipasti* as well.

Pesto is an uncooked sauce that allows the intoxicating bouquet of basil to blossom with pignoli (pine nuts) and garlic. Another sauce called for in Italian cooking, as well as French, is Maionese, or oil and lemon juice thickened with egg.

It is the Italian craftsman who joins these sauces with the fresh ingredients of the season to build a masterpiece. We invite you to do the same.

Tomato sauce and pasta seem an inseparable pair, and yet this was not always the case. During the Renaissance, pasta was eaten with Parmesan and sugar! It wasn't until tomatoes were brought back from the New World that this sauce became popular.

We feel that everyone should have a favorite and reliable tomato sauce recipe to draw on, so we've given you three to choose from. Of these, one has Parmesan and two have a little sugar. All are delicious.

If the sauces are to be served with pasta, begin to boil the water on top of the stove during the last 15 to 20 minutes of cooking time.

Salsa di Pomodoro I
TOMATO SAUCE I

Quantity: about 2 ½ cups   **Cooking time: 25 minutes**

2 tablespoons olive oil
⅔ cup finely chopped onion,
   about 1 medium-size
⅔ cup peeled and finely chopped
   carrot, about 1 medium-size
⅔ cup finely chopped celery

2 pounds red ripe tomatoes,
   preferably plum, or 2 cups
   undrained canned, chopped
¼ teaspoon sugar
½ teaspoon salt

In a 3-quart microwave casserole combine oil, onion, carrot, and celery. Cook on High for 5 minutes, until vegetables are slightly tender, stirring once.

Meanwhile, wash and quarter tomatoes. Add tomatoes, along with sugar and salt, to cooked onion mixture. Cook on High for 10 minutes, stirring once.

Force the tomatoes through a food mill to remove skins. Return to cooking casserole and cook on High for an additional 15 to 20 minutes, stirring occasionally. Allow to stand for 5 minutes before serving.

Salsa di Pomodoro II
TOMATO SAUCE II

A pure, sweet tomato sauce that is delicious served over gnocchi.

Quantity: about 2 cups   Cooking time: 30 minutes

2 pounds red ripe tomatoes,   1 medium-size onion, peeled and
   preferably plum, washed and   halved
   quartered, or 2 cups undrained   ¼ teaspoon sugar
   canned, chopped   ½ teaspoon salt
2 tablespoons butter

Place tomatoes in a 3-quart microwave casserole. Cook on High for 10 minutes. Force the tomatoes through a food mill to remove skins. Return the purée to casserole and add remaining ingredients. Cook on High for 15 to 20 minutes, stirring occasionally. Discard onion.
    Allow to stand for 5 minutes before serving.

Salsa di Pomodoro III
TOMATO SAUCE III

Grated Parmesan cheese is used as a thickening agent in this sauce, and with its addition the cooking power is reduced. Fresh basil instead of dried will make a noticeable flavor difference so, if possible, make this sauce during basil season, and freeze it.

Quantity: about 2 cups   Cooking time: 15 minutes

1 tablespoon olive oil   2 tablespoons chopped parsley
2 garlic cloves, minced   ½ teaspoon salt
2 pounds red ripe tomatoes,   Freshly ground pepper
   preferably plum, peeled,   2 tablespoons grated Parmesan
   seeded, and chopped, or 2   cheese
   cups undrained canned,   2 teaspoons chopped fresh basil
   chopped   or ¼ teaspoon crushed dried

In a 2-quart microwave casserole, combine oil and garlic. Cook on High for 1½ minutes, or until garlic is tender but not brown. Add tomatoes, parsley, salt, and pepper to taste. Cook on High for 8 minutes, stirring halfway through cooking.
    Stir in remaining ingredients and cook on Medium (50% power) for 5 minutes, or until sauce has thickened, stirring occasionally. Allow to stand for 5 minutes before serving.

Ragu alla Bolognese
TOMATO SAUCE WITH MEAT

This sauce hails from Bologna in the north, where beef is more plentiful and affordable than in the south.

Quantity: about 3½ cups   **Cooking time: 30 minutes**

1 tablespoon butter
1 tablespoon olive oil
2 tablespoons chopped onion
2 tablespoons finely chopped
  celery
2 tablespoons chopped, peeled
  carrot
1 pound lean ground beef
¼ cup dry red wine

2 pounds red ripe tomatoes,
  preferably plum, peeled,
  seeded, and chopped, or 2
  cups undrained canned,
  chopped
1 tablespoon tomato paste
½ teaspoon salt
⅛ teaspoon freshly ground
  pepper

In a 3-quart microwave casserole with lid, combine butter, oil, onion, celery, and carrot. Cover and cook on High for 2 minutes, or until vegetables are slightly tender, stirring once.

Add beef, breaking it up into small pieces with a fork. Cook, uncovered, on High for 3 to 5 minutes. Break meat up into even smaller pieces with a fork and stir in wine. Cook, uncovered, for 5 minutes more, stirring once.

Stir in tomatoes, tomato paste, salt, and pepper. Cover and cook on High for 5 minutes. Stir; re-cover and cook on *Medium* (50% power) for 15 to 20 minutes. Stir and allow to stand for 5 minutes before serving.

Ragu alla Casalinga
HOME-STYLE TOMATO MEAT SAUCE

Convenience seems to characterize the American home, so we call this sauce "home-style" because it can be prepared from start to finish in a little over 30 minutes. You can vary the sauce each time, by adjusting the proportions of beef and sausage.

Quantity: about 5½ cups   **Cooking time: 27 minutes**

½ pound Salsiccie con Seme di Finocchi (see Index), or Italian sausage, sweet or hot
½ pound lean ground beef
2 tablespoons olive oil
2 garlic cloves, minced
1 onion, chopped
1 can (28 ounces) Italian plum tomatoes, undrained and chopped

1 can (6 ounces) tomato paste
¼ cup chopped fresh parsley, or 1 tablespoon dried
1 teaspoon chopped fresh basil, or ¼ teaspoon crushed dried
½ teaspoon sugar
½ teaspoon salt
¼ teaspoon red pepper flakes (optional)
Freshly ground black pepper

If using prepared sausage, remove casing. Break up sausage and ground beef. Place a microwave roasting rack in a 2-quart microwave dish (12 x 8") and spread sausage and beef evenly on top. Cook on High for 5 minutes to cook partially, rotating dish once. Drain and set aside.

In a 3-quart microwave casserole with lid, combine oil, garlic, and onion. Cover and cook on High for 2 minutes until vegetables are slightly tender. Stir in cooked meats and remaining ingredients with black pepper to taste. Cover and cook on High for 20 minutes until bubbly hot, stirring twice. Allow to stand, covered, for 5 minutes.

Salsa Balsamella
WHITE SAUCE

With this simple recipe you can create a thin, medium, or thick white sauce. The secret to a good white sauce is to bring the ingredients to a boil and then cook them until thickened to eliminate any raw flour taste.

For use in Lasagne Verde, the recipe must be tripled, so follow variation below.

Quantity: about 1 cup　　　　　　**Cooking time: 5 to 8 minutes**

3 tablespoons butter　　¼ teaspoon salt
3 tablespoons flour　　　⅛ teaspoon white pepper
1 cup milk

Place butter in a 4-cup glass measure; cook on High for 30 seconds to 1 minute, or until melted. Stir in flour to make a smooth paste. Pour in milk and add seasonings, stirring to blend. Cook on High for 5 to 7 minutes until sauce is boiling and thickened, stirring three times.

VARIATIONS　　For a thinner sauce, reduce butter and flour to 2 tablespoons each, and follow basic recipe.

For a thicker sauce, increase butter and flour to 4 tablespoons each, and follow basic recipe.

For Lasagne Verde, follow basic method but increase cooking time and ingredients to yield 3½ cups sauce. In a 2-quart microwave dish, place 4 ounces butter and cook on High for 1½ to 2 minutes. Stir in ½ cup flour and pour in 3 cups milk, adding ¾ teaspoon salt and ¼ teaspoon white pepper. Cook on High for 8 to 10 minutes, until boiling and thickened, stirring three times.

Maionese
MAYONNAISE

Quantity: 1 cup   Preparation time: 5 minutes

1 large egg   1 cup oil (preferably ½ cup olive
¼ teaspoon salt   and ½ cup salad oil)
1 to 2 tablespoons lemon juice

Blender or processor method:
In the bowl of blender or processor, combine egg, salt, and lemon juice; process to blend. As processor is running, pour oil through the feed tube in a slow steady stream. With blender, add ¼ cup oil at a time and blend. Once oil has been added the consistency will be thick and creamy.
By hand:
In a medium-size bowl, combine ingredients in the same order as above, beating with fork or whisk after each addition. Pour oil in a slow steady stream, beating constantly.
Keep refrigerated.

VARIATION   For Maionese con Acciuga e Capperi, Mayonnaise with Anchovies and Capers, add 1 tablespoon finely chopped anchovy fillets, 1 tablespoon drained capers, and 1 tablespoon finely chopped parsley to basic recipe; stir to blend.

Pesto
UNCOOKED BASIL SAUCE

Quantity: about 2 cups   Preparation time: 5 minutes with
                                                  food processor

2 cups firmly packed fresh basil   ½ cup grated Parmesan cheese
   leaves with stems removed   2 tablespoons grated Pecorino
¼ cup pignoli (pine nuts) or   Romano or Parmesan cheese
   walnuts   ½ cup olive oil
2 garlic cloves, peeled

In the bowl of a food processor or blender, combine basil, pignoli, and garlic; chop fine. Add cheeses and blend. Slowly pour in oil, while blending if using a processor, and continue to blend until a fine paste forms.
Pesto will keep refrigerated for 3 days, or may be frozen in individual heavy-duty plastic bags or jars.

SERVING SUGGESTIONS   Pesto may be served over 1 pound cooked pasta, or over Gnocchi (see Index). Before draining pasta or gnocchi, reserve 2 tablespoons of cooking water and add to pesto. Toss with cooked and drained pasta or gnocchi.

Salsa Verde
GREEN (PARSLEY) SAUCE

This is pungent sauce that wonderfully accents leftover meats and poached fish. Traditionally made with a mortar and pestle, we find the food processor an excellent modern-day substitute. Although anchovies add pungence, they are not intrusive and blend quite well with the other ingredients.

Quantity: 1½ cups   **Preparation time: 5 minutes**

1 garlic clove, minced, or peeled
  for processor
1 cup finely chopped fresh
  parsley, or 1¼ cups
  unchopped for processor
6 anchovy fillets, chopped fine, or
  whole for processor

2 tablespoons capers, chopped
  fine, or whole for processor
  (optional)
2 tablespoons lemon juice
½ cup olive oil

Processor method:
    While processor is running, drop garlic through the feed tube to mince. Add parsley; chop fine. Add anchovies and capers; process to mince by pulsing machine frequently. Pour in lemon juice; process and scrape bowl. As processor is running, pour oil through feed tube in a slow steady stream until blended. The consistency will be that of an oil dressing.

By hand:
    In a medium-size bowl, combine minced garlic, chopped parsley, anchovies, and capers; stir to mix. Pour in lemon juice; stir. Pour in oil in a slow steady stream, beating constantly with a wire whisk. The consistency will be that of an oil dressing.

SERVING SUGGESTIONS   Serve with Branzino en Bianco, Chilled Poached Bass in White Wine (see Index).
    Salsa Verde makes a tangy salad dressing, too.

5
Pasta e Farinacei
Pasta, Rice, Gnocchi, and Polenta

One day, hundreds of years ago, a young Chinese maiden was busy preparing her daily batch of bread dough. An ardent Italian sailor engaged her in conversation, and she forgot her task. Soon dough overflowed from the pan, dripping in strings which quickly dried in the sun. The young Italian, hoping to hide the evidence of his loved one's carelessness, gathered the strings of dried dough and took them to his ship. The ship's cook boiled them in broth, and was pleased to find that the dish was appetizing and savory. When the ship returned to Italy, word of the delicious new dish spread rapidly and soon was popular throughout the land. (Paraphased from National Macaroni Institute.)

Unfortunately this lovely story is no more than a folk tale. The reference seems to be to Marco Polo, who is often given credit for bringing pasta from China to Italy. But the fact is that macaroni is referred to in a historical document dated 1200 A.D., at least 50 years before Marco Polo was born!

The words macaroni and lasagna are Greek or Latin in origin. In antiquity, *makaria* was a Greek food served at funeral banquets, and *laganum* was the Latin word for sauce pan noodles. The Chinese probably also had a form of pasta. Yet we must give credit to the Italians, if not for the invention of pasta, at least for their ability to raise what is no more than flour and water or eggs to the heights of gastronomic splendor.

Giuseppe Prezzolini says in his book *Spaghetti Dinner* (New York: Abelard-Schuman, 1955), "Only a people gifted with great fantasy and accustomed to meeting fantasy daily could have found so many forms for the most common food." We are all familiar with spaghetti, or "little strings," and the flat ribbon noodles known as fettuccine. But when ordering a multisyllabled pasta in Italy, you might be asking for little ears, ladies' curls, worms, car radiators, butterflies, tempests, or greedy priests. In this chapter we have been conservative, suggesting only a limited variety of shapes. However, we encourage you to let your fancy run free in order to add a spark of humor, if not enchantment, to your pasta eating experience.

Any pasta may be cooked in the microwave, but we prefer the *al dente* doneness that is best achieved on top of the conventional stove. For this reason we have given you microwave instructions for the sauces but conventional methods for cooking the pasta. Our suggestion is to make these sauces in the microwave while the spaghetti is boiling on the stove.

The same is true of Gnocchi (pronounced "nuckie"), the small potato dumplings. The potatoes for making gnocchi are cooked in the microwave for a dough that, we feel, has a more manageable consistency than when cooked by conventional means (not too dry or soggy). Ultimately, though, the gnocchi should be cooked, conventionally, in boiling water.

The exception to all of this is a dish based on Pasta Verde, Spinach Pasta Dough. The fresh dough strips can be layered, uncooked, in a lasagne casserole and gently steamed by the sauces that envelop them.

We then come to risotto, which will either be an unknown quantity to you or a mouth-watering memory. Risotto is a creamy rice dish, not to be confused with rice pilaf, which takes the place of pasta in areas of northern Italy. For those who might have been leery of attempting risotto before, the microwave provides the simplest and most reliable cooking method we know.

Finally there is polenta, which is as old as the Roman culture itself. With the introduction of corn to Italy from America, northern Italians have turned from millet to make this solid porridge of cornmeal. It is a first course, served either plain or with a sauce, or as an accompaniment for poultry or game.

Pasta all'Uovo
EGG PASTA DOUGH

This dough can be made by hand or with a food processor. When a food processor is used, no kneading is required.

Quantity: ½ pound pasta   Preparation time: 10 to 20 minutes

2 cups semolina or all-purpose   *3 large eggs, lightly beaten*
  flour

Processor method:
     Combine both ingredients in the bowl of a food processor; process until a ball is formed that is moist yet workable, 30 to 45 seconds. If dough is sticky, add 1 tablespoon of flour at a time, processing lightly until the proper consistency is reached. No kneading is necessary.
By hand:
     Place flour in a mound on a flat work surface. Carve out a well in the center with your hands. Add eggs to the center of the well. Using your hand in a circular motion, begin to draw flour from the inside of the well into the eggs. Use the other hand to hold the flour wall in shape. When the eggs are no longer runny, push the rest of the flour over them to cover. Gather the mass into a ball, using a dough scraper. Add more flour, if necessary. Dough should be resilient and slightly sticky.
     Clean the work surface and knead dough by pressing ball forward with the heel of your hand. Fold dough back over in half and rotate one quarter turn. Repeat process until dough is elastic and smooth, 8 to 10 minutes.
     Roll out dough through a pasta machine, or flatten into a 6-inch circle on a well-floured, flat work surface. Roll from the center of the circle, forward, then stretch dough by pushing the rolling pin forward and pulling the dough from behind. After each roll and stretch, turn the dough one quarter turn. Turn dough over and flour surface as necessary. Roll into a large circle, approximately 20 inches across and ⅛ inch thick.
     Cut dough into various thicknesses for different pastas:
● ⅟₁₆-inch strips for Tagliarini
● ⅛-inch strips for Fettuccine
● ¼-inch strips for Tagliatelle
● 3½-inch strips for Lasagne
     Spread noodles out on a cloth towel to dry for a few minutes.
     To cook fresh noodles: Use 4 quarts of water for every pound of pasta. Bring water to a boil in a large pasta pot on top of the stove.

Add 1 tablespoon salt. Add pasta after the water has returned to a boil. Cook for 5 to 10 seconds, stirring with a wooden spoon to prevent sticking; drain.

TIPS   Pasta should be rolled on wood for best results. Marble is too cold to use and will make dough less elastic. Roll quickly; do not allow dough to dry out.

A pasta machine will make rolling easier.

To store noodles: Fold fresh noodles in half or curl a handful around your fingers into a doughnut shape. Allow to dry for 24 hours. Store in tightly sealed wide-mouth glass or plastic jars for up to 1 month, or freeze in moistureproof plastic bags for 3 months.

Pasta Verde
SPINACH PASTA DOUGH

This recipe can be made with a food processor or by hand, and both methods are given. Once the dough has formed a resilient ball, either in the processor or by hand kneading, the rolling out process will be the same.

Quantity: ½ pound pasta   **Preparation time: 10 to 20 minutes**

½ pound fresh spinach leaves, or   1½ cups semolina or all-purpose
*   5 ounces frozen chopped   flour, plus more if necessary*
*   spinach (see Tips)   2 large eggs, lightly beaten*
¼ teaspoon salt

Place fresh spinach or frozen spinach in a 2-quart microwave casserole with lid. Sprinkle with salt. Cover and cook on High for 3 to 4 minutes, until tender, stirring occasionally. Allow to cool under running water, until you can squeeze spinach dry with your hands to eliminate excess moisture.

Processor method:

Place cooked and squeezed-dry spinach in the bowl of a food processor; chop fine. Add flour and eggs and process just until a ball is formed, one that is moist yet workable, 30 to 45 seconds. If dough is

too sticky, add up to ½ cup flour, 1 tablespoon at a time, and process just until the proper consistency is reached. No kneading is necessary.
By hand:
Place flour in a mound on a flat work surface. Carve out a well in the center with your hands. Chop spinach and add with eggs to the center; carefully blend with a fork, keeping mixture away from flour.

Using your hand in a circular motion, begin to draw flour from the inside of the well into the egg-spinach mixture. Use one hand to hold the flour wall in shape while the other hand mixes. When the eggs are no longer runny, push the rest of the flour over to cover. Gather the mass into a ball, using a dough scraper. Add more flour, if necessary. Dough should be resilient and slightly sticky.

Clean the work surface and knead dough by pressing ball forward with the heel of your hand. Fold dough back over in half and rotate one quarter turn. Repeat process until dough is elastic and smooth, 8 to 10 minutes.

Roll out dough through a pasta machine, or flatten into a 6-inch circle on a well-floured, flat work surface. Roll from the center forward, turning the dough one quarter turn after each roll. Turn dough over and flour surface as necessary to make rolling easier. Roll into a large circle, approximately 20 inches across, and ⅛ inch thick or less. Cut circle into *six* 3½- by 10-inch strips, piecing together if necessary. Save remainder of dough and cut into small strips to use in soup.

Use in recipes Lasagne Verde, Lasagne al Ragu (see Index for pages).

TIPS   If only a 10-ounce package of frozen spinach is available, half can be cooked and the other half refrozen. To do this: remove frozen spinach from box and wrap half in aluminum foil, pressing tightly against spinach so that no sharp edges protrude.

Place spinach in a 2-quart microwave casserole with lid. Cover and cook on High for 2 minutes. Cut uncovered defrosted half from frozen half wrapped in foil. Completely cover foil-wrapped half and place back in freezer. Re-cover defrosted spinach in casserole and add salt. Cook for 2 to 3 minutes more, until spinach is completely cooked, stirring occasionally.

If using a pasta machine, slightly less flour will be needed to make the dough.

Ravioli
STUFFED PASTA SQUARES

Quantity: 24 squares   **Preparation time: 30 to 45 minutes**

Pasta all'Uovo, Egg Pasta Dough,   *Cheese or Sausage Filling*
* or Pasta Verde, Spinach Pasta*   *(following recipes)*
* Dough (see Index for pages)*   *1 egg, beaten*
1 tablespoon milk

When mixing basic pasta dough, add 1 tablespoon milk to eggs.

After processing or kneading, divide dough into halves and roll into 2 rectangles, each 7 x 5½ inches. Roll and stretch according to basic pasta recipe, but try to keep dough in 2 rectangular shapes. (A pasta machine will make rolling easier and the size gauged by the machine will determine how many sheets are made.)

Using a tablespoon, place 24 mounds of filling, 1 inch apart, in even rows on one of the dough rectangles.

Brush 1 side of the remaining dough with beaten egg and place, egg side down, on the dough with filling. Press firmly around the filling to seal.

Cut dough evenly between mounds to form 24 squares, using a pasta cutter, sharp knife, or pastry wheel. Lay ravioli on a cloth towel to dry for a few minutes.

Bring 4 quarts of water to a boil on top of the conventional stove. Add ravioli and cook for 5 to 10 minutes until done.

Serve with melted butter and freshly chopped sage or any Salsa di Pomodoro, Tomato Sauce (see Index for pages).

RAVIOLI FILLINGS

Salsiccie
SAUSAGE FILLING

Quantity: about 2 cups   **Cooking time: 15 minutes**

*1½ pounds Salsiccie con
  Parmigiano Prezzemolo,
  Sausage with Cheese and
  Parsley (see Index), or
  packaged sausage with casings
  removed*

*⅓ cup dry bread crumbs
2 egg yolks, beaten*

Place sausage in a 2-quart microwave dish, 12 x 8 inches. Cook on High for 10 to 15 minutes, stirring every 4 minutes until meat has lost pink color. Drain fat. Allow to cool.

In a mixing bowl, combine cooked sausage with bread crumbs and egg yolks.

Ricotta
RICOTTA CHEESE FILLING

Quantity: about 2 cups   **Preparation time: 5 minutes**

*1½ cups ricotta cheese
¼ cup grated Parmesan cheese
½ cup finely chopped fresh
   parsley
1 egg yolk*

Combine all ingredients in a mixing bowl.

Lasagne Verde
GREEN LASAGNE WITH MEAT AND WHITE SAUCES

This classic lasagne dish is rich, yet understated. It will not overwhelm you with pungent cheese and tomato sauce. You will probably reserve it for special company, because of the two homemade sauces and homemade noodles that are involved. The rewards will outweigh the time you spend on it, though. This is a casserole that will make a lasting impression upon your guests when offered as a first or main course.

Servings: 6   Preparation time: 1½ to 2 hours, including all sauces and pasta

3½ cups Ragu alla Bolognese, Tomato Sauce with Meat (see Index)
3½ cups Salsa Balsamella, White Sauce (see Index)

½ pound Pasta Verde, Spinach Pasta Dough (see Index) or fresh lasagne noodles, uncooked
¾ cup grated Parmesan cheese

Pour ½ cup *ragu* into the bottom of a 2-quart microwave dish 12 x 8 inches; spread out evenly. Cover with 2 strips of pasta and spread 1 cup *ragu* evenly on top. Spread 1 cup white sauce on top; sprinkle with ¼ cup grated cheese. Continue layering pasta, *ragu*, white sauce, and grated cheese 2 more times. End second layer with remaining 1½ cups white sauce, sprinkled with grated cheese.

Cover with vented plastic wrap and cook on Medium (50% power) for 20 to 23 minutes, or until noodles are tender and sauce is bubbly, rotating twice.

Allow to stand, covered, for 5 minutes before serving.

Wine Selection: Chianti Classico Riserva or Orvieto Secco

VARIATION   Dry lasagne noodles may be substituted for the fresh and should be added *uncooked*. The cooking time should be increased to 30 or 35 minutes. The texture of the cooked noodles will be firmer than that of the fresh noodles.

TIPS   We found it best to try to dovetail the cooking times for meat sauce and spinach pasta. Before putting the *ragu* in for the final cooking step, cook the spinach to make the pasta during that final cooking time for the *ragu*.

Fresh pasta usually only takes 10 seconds to cook once it is placed in boiling water. That is why we recommend fresh pasta for this recipe and place it *uncooked* in the microwave dish. Covering the lasagne allows the moisture from the sauces to cook the noodles.

If you freeze the casserole, reheat it, covered with plastic wrap, on High for 10 minutes, then on Medium (50% power) for 30 to 40 minutes, until the bottom of the dish feels warm. Shield corners with foil if they begin to overcook.

Spaghetti con Salsa alla Carrettiera
SPAGHETTI WITH FRESH TOMATO AND BASIL SAUCE

This sauce is named for the Italian cartdrivers, who deliver the fresh tomatoes and basil. As any *carrettiere* will tell you, the ingredients must be fresh. We've allowed for a tomato substitute, but the basil must always be right off the cart!

Servings: 4   Cooking time: 7 minutes

1 pound spaghetti or other pasta
2 tablespoons olive oil
2 garlic cloves, minced
2 pounds red ripe tomatoes, preferably plum, peeled, seeded, and chopped, or 2 cups undrained canned, chopped

1 cup fresh basil leaves, stems removed and chopped fine
¼ teaspoon salt
⅛ teaspoon freshly ground pepper

Bring water to boil on top of conventional stove and cook pasta until *al dente*, or still firm to the bite.

Meanwhile, in a 2-quart microwave casserole combine oil and garlic. Cook on High for 45 seconds to 1 minute, or until garlic is tender but not brown. Add tomatoes and basil. Cover with wax paper and cook on High for 5 to 6 minutes, stirring halfway through cooking.

Drain spaghetti and place in serving bowl. Pour sauce over and toss well. Serve immediately.

Wine Selection: Corvo Rosso

TIP   To retain a garden-picked fresh flavor the sauce is covered with wax paper and cooked for only a short period of time.

Lasagne al Ragu

LASAGNE WITH SAUSAGE-MEAT SAUCE AND RICOTTA CHEESE

Uncooked lasagne noodles are layered between ricotta and mozzarella cheeses and *ragu* sauce for this familiar lasagne favorite.

Servings: 6

Cooking time: 35 to 40 minutes including all sauces

5½ cups Ragu alla Casalinga, Home-Style Tomato-Meat Sauce (see Index), or prepared meat sauce
½ pound lasagne noodles, uncooked

15 ounces ricotta cheese
8 ounces mozzarella cheese, sliced thin
¾ cup grated Parmesan cheese

Pour 1 cup *ragu* into the bottom of a 2-quart microwave dish 12 x 8 inches, and spread evenly. Top with the following in this order:
- Single layer of noodles
- 1½ cups *ragu*
- 7½ ounces ricotta cheese, spread evenly
- 4 ounces mozzarella cheese slices, to cover
- 3 tablespoons Parmesan cheese, sprinkled on top
- Single layer of noodles

Complete this process one more time. Top final layer of noodles with 1½ cups *ragu*. Sprinkle top with remaining 3 tablespoons Parmesan cheese.

Cover with vented plastic wrap and cook on Medium (50% power) for 35 to 40 minutes, or until noodles are tender and sauce is bubbly, rotating twice.

Allow to stand, covered, for 5 minutes before serving.

Wine Selection: Aglianico del Vulture

TIP   There is a reason for layering the casserole the way we did. It is to allow the more delicate cheeses, like ricotta and mozzarella, to be on the inside and thus cook by a slower conduction of heat.

As with Lasagne Verde, this dish is cooked on Medium power to cook the pasta more gently. To freeze and reheat later, follow reheat instructions under Tips for Lasagne Verde (see Index).

Spaghetti al Tonno
SPAGHETTI WITH TUNA SAUCE

Servings: 4   Cooking time: 10 minutes

1 pound spaghetti or other pasta
2 tablespoons olive oil
1 garlic clove, minced
1½ cups coarsely chopped red
   ripe tomatoes, preferably
   plum, or canned undrained,
   chopped

2 tablespoons finely chopped
   fresh parsley
1 can (7½ ounces) tuna, drained
¼ teaspoon salt
⅛ teaspoon freshly ground
   pepper

Bring water to a boil on top of conventional stove and cook spaghetti until *al dente*, or still firm to the bite.

Meanwhile, in a 1½-quart microwave casserole, combine olive oil and garlic. Cook on High for 1 minute, until garlic is tender but not brown. Stir in tomatoes and parsley. Cook for 5 to 6 minutes more, stirring once.

Add tuna, salt, and pepper. Cook on High for 2 to 3 minutes, or until sauce is heated through, stirring once.

Drain spaghetti and place in a serving bowl. Pour sauce over and toss well. Serve immediately. Traditionally, no cheese is served at the table with this sauce.

Wine Selection: Dolcetto d'Alba or Verdicchio Classico

Color page one: Antipasti (clockwise from left rear) Peperoni Arrosti e Funghi all'Olio (Roasted Pepper and Mushroom Salad), Verduri Marinati (Marinated Vegetables), Carciofi Ripieni (Stuffed Artichokes), Pomodori con Prosciutto e Basilico (Tomatoes with Prosciutto and Basil), Insalata di Riso (Rice Salad)

Color page two: Zuppa di Frutta di Mare (Fish and Shellfish Soup)

Color page three: Chicken (clockwise from left rear) Petti di Pollo con Castagne (Breaded Chicken Cutlets with Chestnut Stuffing), Petti di Pollo alla Marsala (Breaded Chicken Cutlets with Marsala), Petti di Pollo alla Parmigiana (Breaded Chicken Cutlets with Cheese and Tomato Sauce)

Color page four: Arrosto di Maiale di Capodimonte (Stuffed Rolled Pork Roast of Capodimonte) on a bed of fresh rosemary

Spaghetti alle Vongole
SPAGHETTI IN RED CLAM SAUCE

Servings: 4   **Cooking time: 20 minutes**

2 tablespoons olive oil
2 garlic cloves, minced
1 small onion, chopped fine
1 pound spaghetti or other pasta
2 pounds red ripe tomatoes,
    preferably plum, peeled,
    seeded, and chopped, or 2
    cups undrained canned,
    chopped
2 tablespoons chopped fresh
    basil, or ½ teaspoon crushed
    dried

3 tablespoons chopped fresh
    parsley
⅛ teaspoon freshly ground
    pepper
2 dozen Little Neck clams,
    washed and scrubbed, or 2
    cans (6½ ounces, each),
    drained

In a 3-quart microwave casserole with lid, combine oil, garlic, and onion. Cover and cook on High for 1 to 2 minutes, or until onion is slightly tender.

Meanwhile, bring water to a boil on top of conventional stove and cook pasta until *al dente*, or still firm to the bite.

Add tomatoes, basil, parsley, and pepper to onion mixture. Cook on High for 5 minutes, stirring once. If fresh clams are used, add clams and cover. Cook on High for 7 to 12 minutes, or until clams have opened, stirring occasionally. If canned clams are used, add to cooked tomato mixture, cover, and cook on High for 2 to 3 minutes until hot, stirring occasionally.

Drain spaghetti and place in a serving bowl. Pour sauce over and toss well. Serve immediately. Traditionally, no cheese is served at the table with this dish.

Wine Selection: Barbera d'Alba or Verdicchio Classico

TIP   The tomato sauce is covered to hold steam in, which helps to cook the clams.

Spaghetti al Polpette al Sugo
SPAGHETTI IN MEATBALL SAUCE

Servings: 4 to 6   **Cooking time: 25 minutes**

Meatballs:
1 pound lean ground beef (or
  combined beef, pork, and veal,
  if desired)
1 medium-size onion, chopped
  fine
¼ cup fine dry bread crumbs
2 tablespoons grated Parmesan
  cheese
2 tablespoons finely chopped
  parsley
1 egg, lightly beaten
½ teaspoon salt
¼ teaspoon crushed dried
  orégano
⅛ teaspoon freshly ground
  pepper

Sauce:
1 tablespoon olive oil
1 garlic clove, minced
1 medium-size onion, chopped
  fine
2 cups peeled and quartered red
  ripe tomatoes, preferably
  plum, or undrained canned,
  chopped
2 tablespoons dry red wine
2 tablespoons chopped parsley
½ teaspoon crushed dried
  orégano
½ teaspoon salt
Freshly ground pepper

1 pound spaghetti, cooked

In a medium-size bowl, combine all meatball ingredients. Mix well to blend. Shape into 2-inch meatballs and arrange toward the outside of a microwave roasting rack placed in a 2-quart microwave dish (12 x 8 inches). Cook on High for 6 to 8 minutes, or until meatballs are partially cooked, turning over and repositioning halfway through. Drain and set aside.

Prepare sauce: Combine oil, garlic, and onion in a 2-quart microwave casserole. Cook on High for 1½ minutes, until onion is slightly tender. Add remaining sauce ingredients, and cook on High for 4 minutes, stirring once.

Add meatballs to sauce. Cover with lid or vented plastic wrap and cook on *Medium* (50% power) for 15 minutes, stirring once.

Drain spaghetti and place in a serving bowl. Pour sauce over and toss well. Serve immediately.

Wine Selection: Chianti

TIP   Meat sauces are covered to ensure that both meat and sauce heat evenly.

Spaghetti con Salsiccie al Sugo
SPAGHETTI WITH SAUSAGE SAUCE

Servings: 4 to 6

Cooking time: 30 minutes

1 pound Salsiccie con Seme di Finocchi (see Index), or sweet or hot Italian sausage, or a mixture
1 tablespoon olive oil
1 garlic clove, minced
1 medium-size onion, chopped fine
1 can (28 ounces) Italian plum tomatoes, undrained and chopped
1 can (6 ounces) tomato paste
¼ cup chopped fresh parsley, or 1 tablespoon dried

1 teaspoon chopped fresh basil, or ¼ teaspoon crushed dried
½ teaspoon salt
¼ teaspoon freshly ground black pepper
¼ teaspoon sugar
¼ teaspoon red pepper flakes (optional)
1 pound spaghetti, ziti, or other pasta, cooked
Freshly grated Parmesan cheese

If using prepared sausage, remove casing. Cut sausage into 1-inch pieces. Arrange sausage on a microwave roasting rack placed in a 2-quart microwave dish (12 x 8 inches). Cook on High for 5 to 6 minutes, until sausage is partially cooked. Drain and set aside.

In a 3-quart microwave casserole with lid, combine oil, garlic, and onion. Cover and cook on High for 2 minutes, or until onion is slightly tender. Add tomatoes. Stir in remaining ingredients, except pasta and cheese. Add sausage and stir to blend. Cover and cook on High for 20 minutes, stirring twice.

Drain spaghetti and place in a serving bowl. Pour sauce over and toss well. Serve immediately with a sprinkling of cheese.

Wine Selection: Bardolino

Spaghetti con Fegatini al Sugo
SPAGHETTI WITH CHICKEN LIVERS IN SAUCE

Servings: 4 to 6

Cooking time: 27 minutes

1 pound spaghetti or other pasta
2 tablespoons olive oil
1 medium-size onion, chopped
  fine
1 pound chicken livers, rinsed
  and cut into bite-size pieces
1/4 cup dry white wine
2 cups chopped, peeled, and
  seeded tomatoes, or undrained
  canned, chopped

2 tablespoons chopped fresh
  parsley
1 sprig of fresh rosemary or 1/2
  teaspoon crushed dried
1/2 teaspoon salt
1/4 teaspoon freshly ground black
  pepper
1/4 teaspoon red pepper flakes
  (optional)
Freshly grated Parmesan cheese

Bring water to a boil on top of conventional stove and cook pasta until *al dente*, or still firm to the bite.

Meanwhile, in a 2-quart microwave casserole, combine oil and onion. Cook on High for 2 minutes, or until onion is slightly tender. Add livers and wine; stir. Cook on *Medium* (50% power) for 5 minutes, stirring once.

Add remaining ingredients except grated cheese, and cook on Medium for 12 to 15 minutes to heat through and develop flavors, stirring occasionally.

Drain spaghetti and place in a serving bowl. Pour sauce over and toss well. Serve immediately with a sprinkling of cheese.

Wine Selection: Bardolino

Spaghetti all'Aglio e Olio
SPAGHETTI WITH GARLIC AND OIL

This spaghetti is traditionally served at *mezzonotte*, or midnight, after the theater or dancing. It is said to be the only dish that is appropriate at this time of night because of its pure, true flavors.

Servings: 4   **Cooking time: 10 minutes**

1 pound spaghetti or other pasta
1/2 cup olive oil
2 garlic cloves, minced
2 tablespoons chopped fresh
  parsley

1/4 teaspoon salt
Freshly ground pepper, about 1/4
  teaspoon

Bring water to a boil on top of conventional stove and cook pasta until *al dente*, or still firm to the bite.

When pasta is almost cooked, combine oil and garlic in a 2-quart microwave casserole. Cook on High for 1 to 2 minutes, until garlic is tender but not brown. Add parsley, salt, and pepper; stir.

Drain pasta and toss with garlic oil. Serve immediately.

Wine Selection: Greco di Tufo

Fettuccine alla Carbonara
FETTUCCINE WITH CREAM SAUCE AND BACON

This specialty of Rome is typically served over flat ribbon noodles called fettuccine. Once the pasta is cooked it is tossed, in this order, with beaten egg yolks, cream sauce, bacon, and Parmesan cheese. The order is very important to obtain the desired thickly coated, flavorful pasta dish.

Servings: 4   **Cooking time: 10 minutes**

1 pound fettuccine or spaghetti
½ pound sliced lean bacon,
* about 8 slices, or pancetta*
2 tablespoons olive oil
1 tablespoon butter
1 medium-size onion, chopped
* fine*
1 garlic clove, minced

1 cup half and half, or light
* cream*
¼ cup chopped fresh parsley
½ teaspoon salt
Freshly ground pepper, about ¼
* teaspoon*
3 egg yolks, beaten
½ cup grated Parmesan cheese

Bring water to a boil on top of conventional stove and cook fettuccine until *al dente*, or still slightly firm to the bite.

Meanwhile, place bacon between 2 layers of paper towel in a microwave baking dish and cook on High for 4 to 5 minutes, or until crisp. Break into ¼-inch pieces. Set aside.

In a 1-quart microwave casserole, combine oil, butter, onion, and garlic. Cook on High for 2 minutes until onion is slightly tender; stir. Add half and half, parsley, salt, and pepper. Cover with lid or vented plastic wrap and cook on High for 1 to 3 minutes, or until heated through but not boiling.

Beat egg yolks with a wire whisk in a large serving bowl and toss with cooked, drained pasta. Next add heated half and half mixture to coated pasta and toss. Finally, add bacon pieces and grated cheese; toss well.

Serve immediately with freshly ground pepper and additional cheese.

Wine Selection: Valpolicella (red) or Greco di Tufo (white)

TIP   The best carbonara we tasted in Rome was made with a spicy pancetta which can sometimes be found in Italian or specialty stores.

Paglia e Fieno
STRAW AND HAY NOODLES IN CREAM SAUCE

A quick and attractive pasta that can be prepared and served in one dish. The principle used here as in all cream sauces is to add the cream at the end and cook until just heated through.

Servings: 4

Cooking time: 15 minutes, including pasta cooking time

½ pound thin spinach spaghetti or Taglarini (see Index), cooked
½ pound thin white spaghetti or Tagliarini (see Index), cooked
4 ounces unsalted butter

½ cup heavy cream
¼ teaspoon salt
Freshly ground pepper, about ¼ teaspoon
½ cup grated Parmesan cheese

Drain cooked noodles. Set aside.

Place butter in a 2-quart microwave casserole and cook on High for 45 seconds, or until melted. Add cream and cook for 1 to 1½ minutes more, or until heated through but not boiling.

Add drained pasta to the cream and butter; toss well. Add salt and pepper; toss. Add grated cheese and toss again.

Serve immediately with additional grated cheese and freshly ground pepper.

Wine Selection: Soave

VARIATIONS   For Fettuccine Alfredo, substitute 1 pound cooked fettuccine noodles for green and white noodles. Follow basic recipe, adding a pinch of freshly grated nutmeg along with salt and pepper.

For Paglia e Fieno con Piselli, add ½ pound small fresh peas, cooked, or 6 ounces frozen *petits pois*, thawed, to melted butter along with the cream, and cook for 1 additional minute. To cook fresh peas: Place them in a 1-quart microwave casserole and add 2 tablespoons water. Cover with lid or vented plastic wrap and cook on High for 4 to 6 minutes, until peas are tender, stirring halfway through cooking.

For Tortellini con Piselli, make above variation but serve with 1 pound cooked tortellini.

Fettuccine alla Gorgonzola
FETTUCCINE WITH GORGONZOLA SAUCE

Gorgonzola cheese used to be made on a small scale by the regional cheesemakers near Milan. That is when it was known as *stracchino Gorgonzola*, the "tired" cheese, because it was a product of cows weary from the summer's end trek down the Alps.

There is nothing "tired" about the flavor of Gorgonzola, though. It has the characteristic zing of a truly great blue cheese and it imparts that flavor to this pasta dish.

Servings: 4   **Cooking time: 10 minutes**

1 pound fettuccine or spaghetti
4 ounces Gorgonzola cheese, or
   other blue cheese
⅓ cup milk

3 tablespoons butter
¼ cup heavy cream
⅓ cup grated Parmesan cheese

Bring water to a boil on top of conventional stove and cook pasta until *al dente*, or still firm to the bite.

Meanwhile, place Gorgonzola cheese in a 1-quart microwave casserole. Mash cheese with a fork; stir in milk and butter. Cook on Medium (50% power) for 3 to 5 minutes, or until creamy, stirring twice. Set aside.

When pasta is almost *al dente*, add heavy cream to Gorgonzola sauce and cook on Medium for 2 to 4 minutes, until sauce is heated through.

Drain pasta and toss with sauce and grated Parmesan cheese. Serve immediately.

Wine Selection: Cabernet (Grave del Friuli or Collio)

TIP   The power is dropped to Medium to heat the cheese slowly.

Spaghetti con Salsa dell'Olive
SPAGHETTI WITH OLIVE SAUCE

Piquant olives in a creamy rose sauce are an unusual but irresistible combination.

Servings: 4   Cooking time: 8 minutes

1 pound spaghetti or other pasta
¼ cup olive oil
1 garlic clove, minced
½ cup imported black or purple olives (20 to 30), pitted and chopped
¼ pound red ripe tomatoes, preferably plum, peeled and chopped, or ½ cup undrained canned, chopped

2 tablespoons chopped fresh parsley
½ cup half and half
¼ teaspoon pepper
Salt

Bring water to a boil on top of conventional stove and cook pasta until *al dente*, or still firm to the bite.

Meanwhile, in a 1½-quart microwave casserole, combine oil and garlic. Cook on High for 1½ minutes, or until garlic is tender but not brown. Stir in olives and tomatoes. Cook on High for 3 minutes.

Stir in parsley, half and half, pepper, and salt to taste. Cook for 1 to 2 minutes more, or until heated through; stir. Drain pasta and place in a serving bowl. Pour sauce over and toss very well. Serve immediately.

Wine Selection: Corvo Rosso or Montepulciano d'Abruzzo

TIP   Use imported Italian, Greek, or Spanish olives with pits for they have the best flavor. You will find these in specialty stores or the specialty sections of supermarkets.

Pitting olives is made easier with a cherry pitter or paring knife.

Spaghetti Primavera
SPRINGTIME SPAGHETTI WITH VEGETABLES IN CREAM SAUCE

Servings: 4 to 6   Cooking time: 17 minutes

1 pound spaghetti
2 tablespoons olive oil
2 garlic cloves, minced
½ pound red ripe tomatoes,
*   preferably plum, peeled,*
*   seeded, and chopped, or 1 cup*
*   undrained canned, chopped*
1 tablespoon tomato paste
1½ teaspoons finely chopped
*   fresh basil, or ½ teaspoon*
*   crushed dried*
½ cup grated Parmesan cheese
½ cup half and half

2 cups broccoli flowerets (about
*   1 bunch), cut into bite-size*
*   pieces*
2 small zucchini, cut into ¼-inch
*   slices*
2 cups thin-sliced mushrooms
*   (about ¼ pound)*
½ teaspoon salt
¼ teaspoon freshly ground black
*   pepper*
¼ teaspoon red pepper flakes
*   (optional)*

Bring water to a boil on top of conventional stove and cook spaghetti until *al dente*, or still firm to the bite.

Meanwhile, in a 3-quart microwave casserole with lid, combine oil and garlic. Cook on High for 1½ minutes, or until garlic is tender, but not brown. Add tomatoes, tomato paste, and basil. Cook on High for 5 minutes, stirring once.

Stir in grated cheese and half and half. Add broccoli and stir. Cover and cook on High for 3 to 5 minutes, until broccoli is partially cooked, stirring once. Add remaining ingredients; stir well. Cover and cook on High for 4 to 6 minutes, or until heated through but not boiling, stirring once.

Drain spaghetti and place in a serving bowl. Pour sauce over spaghetti and toss well. Serve immediately with additional cheese.

Wine Selection: Orvieto or Gavi

Fettuccine con Salsa di Funghi
FETTUCCINE WITH MUSHROOM SAUCE

Servings: 4   Cooking time: 6 minutes

1 pound fettuccine, green or
  white
2 ounces butter
1 tablespoon flour
1 pound mushrooms, sliced thin
½ cup half and half
2 tablespoons finely chopped
  fresh parsley

2 tablespoons grated Parmesan
  cheese
½ teaspoon salt
¼ teaspoon freshly ground
  pepper

Bring water to a boil on top of conventional stove and cook pasta until *al dente*, or still firm to the bite.

Meanwhile, place butter in a 3-quart microwave casserole and cook on High for 1 to 1½ minutes, until melted. Stir in flour until smooth. Add mushrooms. Cook on High for 2 minutes; stir.

Add remaining ingredients and cook on High for 2 to 3 minutes, or until sauce is heated through.

Stir in cooked and drained fettuccine and toss. Serve with additional grated cheese.

Wine Selection: Pinot Grigio

TIP   This sauce is cooked uncovered to eliminate excess moisture from the mushrooms. A large casserole increases surface area to aid evaporation of moisture.

Maccheroni al Forno
BAKED MACARONI

This is the real Italian version of the kid's favorite, macaroni and cheese. A creamy, tomato-flavored sauce makes it mild yet tasty. Because our kids have fun eating the larger pieces, we have suggested using rigatoni, but choose the size that fits your needs.

Servings: 4   Cooking time: 15 minutes

3 tablespoons butter
1 medium-size onion, chopped
fine
3 tablespoons flour
1 cup milk

½ cup chicken stock
¼ cup tomato paste
¾ cup grated Parmesan cheese
4 cups cooked and drained
rigatoni or other macaroni

In a 2-quart microwave casserole, combine butter and onion. Cook on High for 2 to 2½ minutes or until onion is tender. Stir in flour to form a well-blended paste. Pour in milk, stirring constantly. Add stock and tomato paste, stirring to blend.

Cook on High for 5 to 7 minutes, until sauce comes to a boil and thickens, stirring three times. Stir in ½ cup of cheese.

Fold in the cooked macaroni and sprinkle remaining ¼ cup cheese on top. Cook on *Medium* (50% power) for 8 to 10 minutes, until macaroni is heated through, rotating ½ turn halfway through cooking.

Maccheroni all'Arrabbiata
MACARONI WITH TOMATOES AND HOT PEPPER

Arrabbiata means "mad" or "angry" and refers to the *flaming* taste of the sauce.

Servings: 4 to 6   **Cooking time: 10 minutes**

1 pound macaroni (penne,
tubetti, ditali)
¼ cup olive oil
2 garlic cloves, minced
½ teaspoon red pepper flakes
2 pound red ripe tomatoes,
preferably plum, peeled,
seeded, and chopped, or
2 cups undrained canned,
chopped

¼ teaspoon salt
2 tablespoons chopped parsley

Bring water to a boil on top of conventional stove and cook macaroni until *al dente*, or still firm to the bite.

Meanwhile, in a 2-quart microwave casserole, combine oil, garlic and red pepper. If you like a very "hot" dish, add red pepper flakes to taste. Cook on High for 1 minute, or until garlic is tender, but not brown. Stir in tomatoes and salt. Cook on High for 4 to 5 minutes, stirring once. Add parsley and stir. Cook for 1 to 2 minutes more.

Drain macaroni and fold into tomato-pepper sauce to coat. Cook on High for 1 to 2 minutes, or until macaroni and sauce are heated through, stirring halfway through cooking.

Wine Selection: Barbera, Montepulciano d'Abruzzo, or Sangiovese

Maccheroni al Vodka
MACARONI WITH VODKA SAUCE

This is a quickly prepared creamy, sweet sauce. You will not be assaulted with vodka, but rather notice a richness, as well as a pleasant change from garlic.

Servings: 4   **Cooking time: 10 minutes**

1 pound small macaroni (penne, tubetti)

2 ounces butter

1/2 pound red ripe tomatoes, preferably plum, peeled, seeded, and chopped, or 1/2 cup undrained canned, chopped

3 tablespoons vodka

2 tablespoons chopped parsley

1/3 cup half and half

3/4 cup grated Parmesan cheese

1/4 teaspoon salt

1/8 teaspoon freshly ground pepper

Bring water to a boil on top of conventional stove and cook macaroni until al dente, or still firm to the bite; drain.

Meanwhile, place butter in a 1½-quart microwave casserole. Cook on High for 1½ to 2 minutes. Add tomatoes, vodka, and parsley; stir. Cook on High for 5 minutes, stirring once halfway through cooking.

Stir in half and half, cheese, salt, and pepper. Cook on Medium (50% power) for 2 to 3 minutes, or until heated through. Serve over cooked and drained macaroni.

Wine Selection: Orvieto Abboccato (semi-dry)

Risotto
ITALIAN RICE DISH

Risotto is a heavenly rice dish which lends itself to the creativity of the cook. Being popular in Venice, the city of water, this dish is often described as "shimmering" because that is the way it should be served, still moist and creamy. At the same time the texture should be *al dente*, or still firm in the center. Happily, long-grain rice can be cooked to *al dente*, but we prefer the flavor and texture of Arborio rice.

When risotto is cooked on the conventional stove, heat must be carefully regulated so as not to cook the rice too quickly. Liquid must be added ½ cup at a time, with constant stirring. We found the microwave to be much more consistent in cooking than the conventional stove, and it is done without any stirring. The novice need not be shy and will be pleased at how easy it is to create one of Italy's classic dishes.

Servings: 4 or about 2 ½ cups   **Cooking time: about 15 minutes**

3 tablespoons butter
1 medium-size onion, chopped
   fine
1 cup Italian Arborio rice or
   short-grain rice, or Converted
   long-grain rice

1¾ cups hot chicken stock (just
   boiling)
⅓ cup grated Parmesan cheese

In a 3-quart microwave casserole with lid, combine butter and onion. Cover and cook on High for 1½ to 2 minutes, or until onion is slightly tender. Add rice and stir well to coat with butter. Stir in stock and cover. Cook on High for 4 to 6 minutes, or until stock boils.

Stir and re-cover. Cook on *Medium* (50% power) for 6 to 8 minutes until rice swells, absorbing almost all the liquid, yet remaining firm to the bite. Do not stir during cooking.

Stir in cheese. Re-cover and allow to stand for 5 minutes; during this time rice will continue to cook.

Wine Selection: Northern Italian Chardonnay or Dolcetto

TIP   Stirring rice during cooking will cause it to break up and become starchy.

VARIATION   For Risotto alla Milanese, add ¼ teaspoon crushed saffron threads or ⅛ teaspoon powdered saffron with the rice. Follow basic recipe procedure.

Gnocchi di Patate
SMALL POTATO DUMPLINGS

Gnocchi are potato dumplings that look like small, spiral etched bullets. We think you will find them suprisingly quicker and easier to make than pasta, and with this method the end result will be light, well-shaped gnocchi.

When making gnocchi, cooks are careful to tell you either to bake the potatoes conventionally, or to boil them in water, taking care not to prick the potatoes lest they absorb too much water. The moisture control and quickness of the microwave makes this process a snap.

If you prefer a simpler and guaranteed foolproof method, try the ricotta cheese gnocchi that we have listed as a variation. It was graciously contributed to us by a friend who married into a family of Italians.

Servings: 4 to 6   Preparation time: Depends on proficiency

4 medium-size potatoes,
preferably russet (about 1½
pounds)
¾ cup semolina or all-purpose
flour

1 egg yolk
Freshly grated Parmesan cheese
Sauce (see Serving Suggestions)

Prick unpeeled potatoes with a fork once on top and bottom.

On microwave oven shelf, place a piece of paper towel and position potatoes on top in a circle, allowing 1-inch space between them. Cook on High for 10 to 14 minutes, or until they give slightly when squeezed between the fingers. Allow potatoes to stand for 10 minutes.

Peel potatoes and purée them through a ricer or food mill into a medium-size bowl. Add ¾ cup flour and the egg yolk. Blend with hands to make a smooth dough that is still slightly sticky. If more flour is needed, add it 1 tablespoon at a time until dough reaches the right consistency.

Shape dough into a thick sausage-shaped roll, 2 to 3 inches thick. Cut into 8 pieces. Shape each piece into long finger rolls, 6 to 8 inches by ¾ inch, flouring hands if necessary to roll. Cut each finger roll into ¾-inch pieces.

Turn a fork with the curved back facing you. With your index finger, press each ¾-inch piece of dough against the base of the fork tines. With finger, drag dough along tines from the base to tip, causing dough to fold over finger slightly to form a bullet-shaped roll. That is one. Now follow the same procedure for each piece of dough.

Bring 5 quarts of salted water to boil on top of the stove. Cook 2 dozen gnocchi at a time, boiling for 8 to 10 seconds after they bob to the surface. With a slotted spoon, lift each batch of gnocchi from water and transfer to a heated shallow platter.

Meanwhile, reheat your chosen sauce in microwave and divide cooked gnocchi among individual serving plates or bowls. Sprinkle with grated cheese, then top with heated sauce.

Wine selection: Barbera with tomato sauce, Greco di Tufo with pesto

VARIATION   Combine 1 cup ricotta cheese with 1 cup fine semolina or other flour to make a dough. Use this in place of the potato dough and follow basic recipe method. You will find that this dough is slightly firmer and stickier, so additional flour on your hands may be needed when rolling out and forming gnocchi on tines of fork. Just remember the 1:1 proportion of cheese to flour and you will be able to adapt it to the amounts you have on hand.

SERVING SUGGESTIONS   Serve with Salsa di Pomodoro II, Tomato Sauce II, or Pesto, Uncooked Basil Sauce (see Index for pages).

TIP   Sprinkling the cooked gnocchi with cheese first helps to absorb any excess moisture that may not have drained off.

Polenta

CORNMEAL PORRIDGE

The K-ration of the Roman army was *pulmentum*, or polenta. In those days it was made with some type of wheat, barley or other grain. Today it is made mostly of corn and has acquired a special place in the home cooking in the north of Italy, much as our corn bread has in the southern United States.

Polenta can be most closely compared to a spoon bread: it is used in place of the pasta course or as a side dish for poultry and game. When cooked on top of the conventional stove, polenta takes 40 to 50 minutes of constant slow stirring. The microwave offers a pleasant alternative for those who want to experiment with polenta without the painstaking effort.

Servings: 4 to 8   **Cooking time: 15 minutes**

6 cups water   *2 cups coarse cornmeal*
2 teaspoons salt   *1 tablespoon olive oil*

Combine all ingredients in a 3-quart microwave casserole with lid; mix well.

Cover and cook on High for 10 minutes, stirring well to blend halfway through cooking and at the end of cooking. Re-cover and cook for 4 to 6 minutes more, stirring every 2 minutes, or until water has been absorbed and mixture has the consistency of mashed potatoes.

Pour cooked polenta into a water-moistened wooden salad bowl or rounded shallow platter. Smooth top of mixture. This will shape polenta into a mounded round loaf when turned out. Allow to stand for 5 to 10 minutes, until partially set.

Turn out onto a serving platter. Allow to stand for 2 to 3 minutes. Serve in bowls with sauce or as a side dish.

SERVING SUGGESTIONS: Serve as a first course with Salsa di Pomodoro I, Tomato Sauce I; Ragu alla Bolognese, Tomato Sauce with Meat; Ragu alla Casalinga, Home-Style Tomato-Meat Sauce; or other pasta sauce of your choice (see Index for pages).

TIPS   The water-moistened bowl makes it easier to turn the polenta out.

Leftover polenta can be refrigerated and reheated later to be served with a sauce.

For a quick casserole, layer leftover polenta in slices with about 2 cups tomato sauce, Pesto (see Index) and Parmesan cheese to taste. Cover with vented plastic wrap and cook on Medium (50% power) until hot and bubbly. The cooking time will depend on the amount of polenta left over, but overcooking is practically impossible. Serve with Italian sausage as a Sunday night dinner.

Polenta Formaggio
CHEESE POLENTA

Butter and Parmesan cheese are stirred into basic polenta for a creamier, more flavorful dish that can be served without sauce in place of pasta. As a side dish, its cheesy flavor will enhance a main dish like Cornish Hens Simmered in Gin Sauce.

Servings: 4 to 6   **Cooking time: 15 minutes**

6 cups water
2 teaspoons salt
2 cups coarse cornmeal
1 tablespoon olive oil

4 ounces, butter, cut into 16
   pieces
⅓ cup grated Parmesan cheese

Combine all ingredients except butter and cheese in a 3-quart microwave casserole with lid.

Cover and cook on High for 10 minutes, stirring well to blend halfway through cooking and at the end of cooking. Re-cover and cook for 4 to 6 minutes more, or until water has been absorbed and the mixture has the consistency of mashed potatoes, stirring every 2 minutes.

Stir in butter and cheese. Spoon into individual bowls and serve immediately, with additional grated cheese.

Polenta Pasticciata
POLENTA LAYERED WITH BOLOGNESE SAUCE

In this dish, polenta is layered with Ragu alla Bolognese, Tomato Sauce with Meat, and Parmesan cheese. It is good as an alternative to Lasagne.

Servings: 6 to 8   Cooking time: about 1 hour

Polenta (see Index)   *1 cup grated Parmesan cheese*
3½ cups Ragu alla Bolognese,   *3 ounces butter, melted*
*   Tomato Sauce with Meat (see*
*   Index)*

Prepare polenta and cool. Cover and chill for 1 hour, or until set.
    Prepare Ragu alla Bolognese.
    Cut cold polenta into ¼-inch-thick slices, and divide slices into 3 portions. Place one third of polenta slices in a single layer in a 2-quart microwave dish (12 x 8 inches). Spread polenta with 1 cup *ragu*, sprinkle with ⅓ cup cheese, and drizzle with 2 tablespoons melted butter. Repeat this process 2 more times to make 3 layers. Top with remaining ½ cup *ragu*.
    Cover with vented plastic wrap and cook on Medium (50% power) for 13 to 18 minutes, or until hot and bubbly, rotating dish twice. Allow to stand for 5 minutes before serving.

6
Pizza

Pizza

In Italy, pizza is as popular as you might imagine. In Rome, counter pizza parlors sell pizza with the chewy thicker crust at breakfast. Pizza with thin crispy crust is popular in *trattorie*, or small restaurants, for a late night dinner. We have also enjoyed them with cocktails as an *antipasto* along the Amalfi coast. The latter is what we had in mind when we developed this particular pizza.

The recipe makes 8 individual pizzas that are cooked 4 at a time (the remaining 4 can be cooked later or cooked and frozen for another occasion). We found out the secret to a lighter crust from a friend's Italian grandfather—it was the addition of an egg. We found that baking powder helped, too. Semolina, instead of flour, adds a special flavor and tints the crust to the yellow of the Napoli sun. In addition to delicious flavor and color, the pizza browns and crisps in just minutes on the browning grill.

Pizza Margherita
PIZZA WITH TOMATO AND CHEESE

This very simple pizza with a fresh tomato sauce and cheese seemed to be the most popular of all pizzas in Italy.

Servings: 8 individual pizzas   **Cooking time: about 8 minutes**

77

Dough:
1 package dry yeast
½ cup warm water
4 tablespoons butter
2 cups semolina or all-purpose
   flour
½ teaspoon baking powder
1 egg

Topping:
2 pounds peeled, seeded, and
   chopped ripe tomatoes,
   preferably plum, or 2 cups
   drained canned, chopped
1 tablespoon olive oil
Salt
Pepper
Orégano
8 ounces mozzarella cheese,
   coarsely grated

In a small bowl, dissolve yeast in the warm water.

In a 1-cup glass measure, soften buttter on Warm (10% power) for 1 minute.

Processor method:

In the processor bowl, combine semolina and baking powder; process. Add yeast and water, softened butter, and egg. Process just until a ball of dough forms. Add a little more semolina if dough is too moist. Knead by hand for 3 to 5 minutes, until smooth and silky, adding semolina as necessary.

By hand:

On a clean working surface, combine semolina and baking powder, forming a mound with a well in the center. Combine yeast and water, softened butter, and egg in center of well. With fingertips, gather semolina from sides to the liquid in the well and mix until a ball of dough is formed. Knead for 10 to 15 minutes, until dough is smooth and silky, adding semolina as necessary.

Place kneaded dough in an oiled glass or microwaveproof bowl, large enough to hold a doubled volume of dough. Cover with wax paper. Allow to double in a warm, draft-free place, or in the microwave. To double in microwave, place covered bowl in a dish of hot water. Heat bowl in dish on Warm (10% power) for 4 minutes, rotating once. Let stand for 15 minutes. Repeat process once more, or until dough has doubled.

During the last 15 minutes of standing time, remove dough from oven and prepare tomatoes for topping. In a 1-quart microwave casserole, combine tomatoes and oil. Cook on High for 3 to 5 minutes, until just heated through, stirring once.

When dough has risen, punch it down and divide into 8 equal pieces. Roll each into a 4-inch diameter round.

Meanwhile, place a microwave browning dish in oven and heat according to manufacturer's instructions for pizza, between 3 to 5 minutes on High depending on dish size; a small dish will take less time. Lightly oil the heated dish. Place 2 or 4 pizzas on dish (depending on dish size) and cook on High for 4 minutes. With a metal spatula, transfer pizzas from dish to a glass or metal tray, flipping over, cooked side up. Reheat browning dish for 2 to 4 minutes, the smaller dish for the shorter amount of time.

Meanwhile, top each pizza with ¼ cup tomato sauce. Sprinkle with salt, pepper, orégano, and 1 ounce (or 2 tablespoons) of grated cheese.

Replace pizzas on heated dish. Cook for 4 minutes more, or until cheese melts. Serve pizzas hot.

Remaining pizzas may be cooked in the same way. If you plan to freeze some of them, cook them on 1 side only, top with tomato, seasonings, and cheese; freeze. To cook frozen pizzas: Do not thaw, but heat browning dish according to basic recipe instructions. Cook pizzas on High for 4 minutes, or until cheese melts.

Wine selection: Chianti

VARIATIONS   For Pizza alla Marinara, Tomato-Garlic Pizza, proceed with basic pizza dough. When making tomato topping, combine 2 minced garlic cloves with olive oil. Cook on High for 30 to 45 seconds, until garlic is tender but not brown. Add tomatoes and cook for 3 to 5 minutes.

For Pizza al Funghi, Mushroom Pizza, divide ½ cup thin-sliced mushrooms among 8 pizzas, sprinkling cheese on top before cooking on browning dish.

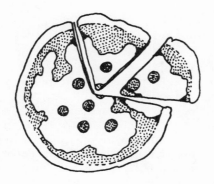

7
Pesce

Fish

A country surrounded by the sea owes much to it. And so there are
many legends that are woven with salt air and sea foam.

·One is a charming story about an Abruzzi man who lived on the
Adriatic Sea. He was a bowlegged old man, who daily donned a black
jacket and a rumpled black hat that seemed to press furrows in his
forehead. This man had many complaints in life: all his sons were
dead, his wife was ailing, and he was poor. One day, when he was
walking through the woods, complaining about his condition, a kindly
old ·man said to him, "I am aware of all your troubles and I will help
you. Here are 100 coins."

The bowlegged man skipped home and hid the coins under a pile
of manure, not telling his wife, who would surely squander them. The
next night the man came home to find a sumptuous feast at his table.
He said, "Wife, how did you pay for such a feast?" She answered, "Why
I sold the pile of manure!" The man was furious and once again lapsed
into moaning and grumbling.

The next day he ambled through the woods again, complaining
even louder than before. A kindly voice said, "I am aware of all your
troubles and I will help you. Here are 100 coins." The joyful man rushed
home to hide the money under the ash pile. Perhaps you can guess
what happened. The next night he feasted well on his wife's meal, but
had lost his money through the sale of the ash pile.

Once again he found the man in the woods who said to him, "This
time I will give you 24 frogs, which you are to sell to buy the biggest
fish you can find." The old man did so and brought home the biggest,

shiniest fish he had ever seen. He hung it on his front porch and it swayed in the sea breezes, shimmering and gleaming in the moonlight.

Now there happened to be a storm that night. A boat of fishermen had lost their bearing and surely would have perished, had they not seen the fish hung out as a lantern. The fishermen came to the old man in black and said, "We will give you half our haul for saving us, and half our haul hereafter if you will but hang out the fish." The old man was never hungry or poor again.*

That fish was the salvation for the Abruzzi man. Fish may well be your salvation at dinnertime because it cooks so quickly in the microwave and is so easy to prepare (with so little waste).

Fish are cooked on High power in the microwave, except for a larger whole fish and the stuffed *calamari* (squids). We have found, though, that High power wattage can vary from oven to oven. The faster cooking ovens may cause the fish to "pop" and cook too quickly. If you find this to be the case, simply reduce the power to Medium (50% power) and adjust by cooking for a few minutes longer, or until the fish flakes.

If you have never tried squid before, there is no time like the present. The Italians have so many wonderful treatments for squid, and we have chosen two: Calamari Ripieni, Stuffed Squid, cooked to tender perfection in a thick tomato sauce, and Calamari al Nino, a spicy dish which is delicious spooned over spaghetti. As we stress everywhere in the book, fresh is better, and that includes squid. If you are unable to get anything but frozen, make sure to rinse it well, inside and out, in cold water to remove any excess salt that collects from the squid sitting longer in its juices.

Pesce alla Senape
FISH FILLETS WITH MUSTARD MAYONNAISE

Very quick and simple to prepare. A favorite with everyone.

Servings: 4   **Cooking time: 10 minutes**

1½ pounds fish fillets (sole, flounder, whiting, scrod)
½ cup Maionese, Mayonnaise (see Index) or commercial mayonnaise

2 tablespoons Dijon-style mustard
1 teaspoon grated lemon rind
Lemon wedges
Freshly chopped parsley

*Paraphrased from Italo Calvino, *Italian Folktales*. Translated by George Martin. New York: Helen and Kurt Wolf Books, Harcourt Brace Jovanovich, 1980.

Place fish on individual microwaveproof serving dishes or arrange in a 2-quart microwave dish (12 x 8 inches), with the thicker edges toward the outside.

In a small bowl, combine mayonnaise, mustard and lemon rind; spread over fish fillets. Cook on High for 7 to 10 minutes, until fish flakes easily, repositioning dishes or rotating dish after 4 minutes.

Garnish with lemon wedges, with a cut side dipped into chopped parsley.

Wine Selection: Verdicchio

TIP   The mayonnaise-mustard sauce acts as a covering for the fish, therefore this dish is not covered.

SERVING SUGGESTIONS   Serve with Cipolline in Agrodolce, Sweet and Sour Green Onions. Begin with Spaghetti Primavera, Springtime Spaghetti (see Index for pages).

Pesce alla Livornese
FISH FILLETS IN TOMATO-CARROT SAUCE

Livorno (Leghorn) is a Tuscan city on the Ligurian Sea. A Livornese-style dish indicates a tomato-garlic sauce.

Servings: 4   Cooking time: 15 to 20 minutes

2 tablespoons olive oil
2 garlic cloves, minced
1 medium-size onion, chopped
   fine
1 small carrot, peeled and
   chopped fine
½ celery rib, chopped fine

1 cup peeled and chopped ripe
   tomatoes, preferably plum, or
   undrained canned, chopped
½ teaspoon salt
⅛ teaspoon freshly ground
   pepper
½ teaspoon orégano, crushed
1½ pounds fish fillets (sole,
   flounder, whiting)

In a 2-quart microwave dish (12 x 8 inches), combine oil, garlic, and onion. Cook on High for 1 to 2 minutes, until onion and garlic are slightly tender. Add remaining ingredients except fish; stir. Cook on High for 8 to 10 minutes, stirring halfway through cooking.

Place fillets in sauce, with thicker edges toward the outside. Cook on High for 7 to 10 minutes, until fish flakes easily, repositioning fish to allow the thicker sections to cook more evenly and rotating dish halfway through cooking.

Serve each fillet with some sauce spooned over it.

Wine Selection: Bianco Vergine

TIP   This fish is not covered because the sauce helps to keep it moist. Covering would keep too much moisture in, resulting in a watery sauce.

SERVING SUGGESTION   Begin with Risotto (see Index).

Branzino Marechiare
SEA BASS COOKED WITH CLAMS IN TOMATO SAUCE

A festive dish that is as delightful to eat as it is to look at.

Servings: 4   Cooking time: 15 to 18 minutes

1 tablespoon olive oil
2 garlic cloves, minced
1 cup peeled and chopped ripe tomatoes, preferably plum, or undrained canned, chopped
1 tablespoon finely chopped parsley
1 tablespoon chopped fresh basil, or ½ teaspoon crushed dried

¼ teaspoon salt
⅛ teaspoon freshly ground pepper
2 pounds (1 or 2 fillets) black sea bass or striped bass
1 dozen Little Neck clams

In a 2-quart microwave dish (12 x 8 inches), combine oil and garlic. Cook on High for 30 to 45 seconds, until garlic is tender but not brown.

Add tomatoes, parsley, basil, salt, and pepper. Cook on High for 5 minutes, stirring once halfway through cooking.

Place fish in the sauce in the center of the dish. Position clams around the outside edge of the dish. Cover with vented plastic wrap. Cook on High for 5 minutes. Turn fish over and reposition clams that have opened with those still shut (this will even out the cooking). Re-cover and cook for 3 to 7 minutes more, or until fish flakes easily and all clams have opened. Allow to stand, covered, for 2 minutes.

To serve: Cut fish into 4 pieces, and serve 1 piece of fish and 3 clams on each individual plate. Spoon sauce over fish.

Wine Selection: Trebbiano d'Abruzzo

SERVING SUGGESTIONS   Begin with spaghetti sauced with Pesto (see Index).

Serve with Broccoli all'Olio e Aglio, Broccoli with Oil and Garlic (see Index).

TIP   Clams are positioned around the outside edge of the dish to receive the large concentration of microwave energy. This allows clams and fish to finish cooking at the same time.

Sogliola al Sambuca
SOLE WITH SAMBUCA

Sambuca is the licorice-flavored liqueur favored in Latium, the area surrounding Rome.

Servings: 4   Cooking time: 15 minutes

1 tablespoon olive oil
1 medium-size onion, chopped
  fine
1 cup peeled and chopped ripe
  tomatoes, preferably plum, or
  undrained canned, chopped
2 tablespoons chopped fresh
  parsley

2 tablespoons Sambuca or other
  licorice-flavored liqueur
¼ teaspoon salt
⅛ teaspoon freshly ground
  pepper
1½ pounds sole fillets, flounder,
  halibut or whiting

In a 2-quart microwave dish (12 x 8 inches), combine oil and onion. Cook on High for 1 minute, or until onion is slightly tender. Stir in remaining ingredients except fish. Cook on High for 5 minutes, stirring once.

Arrange fillets in sauce, with thicker edges toward the outside. Cover with wax paper. Cook on High for 7 to 10 minutes, or until fish flakes easily, repositioning fillets and rotating dish halfway through cooking.

Wine Selection: Est! Est! Est! or Frascati

SERVING SUGGESTION   Serve with Zucchini Rapido, Quick Zucchini (see Index).

TIP   Wax paper is used as a cover to keep some of the steam in during cooking; plastic wrap would hold in too much steam.

Branzino in Bianco
CHILLED POACHED BASS IN WHITE WINE

The bass cooks by microwave energy and the steam of vaporizing juices. Present this whole fish on a platter to make a delicious and dramatic presentation.

Servings: 4 to 6   **Cooking time: 20 to 25 minutes**

¼ cup dry white wine
1 small carrot, sliced thin
1 medium-size onion, sliced thin
½ teaspoon salt
⅛ teaspoon freshly ground
  pepper

2 tablespoons lemon juice
3-pound whole black sea bass or
  striped bass, whole-dressed
  with gills removed but head
  and tail intact

In a large glass or microwave platter, or 3-quart microwave dish (13 x 9 inches), combine all ingredients except fish; stir. Place fish in dish. Cover eye with a strip of aluminum foil folded smoothly around the head. Cover dish with vented plastic wrap. Cook on Medium (50% power) for 20 to 25 minutes, or until fish flakes easily in the thickest part, rotating dish 2 or 3 times. Drain and discard vegetables.

Place fish on a serving platter and chill. Serve with Maionese con Acciuga e Capperi, Mayonnaise with Anchovies and Capers, or with Salsa Verde, Green Sauce (see Index for pages).

Wine Selection: Gavi

VARIATION   Trout can be poached in the same way. Estimate 9 to 12 minutes per pound on Medium power.

SERVING SUGGESTIONS   Place fish on a large serving platter with fresh parsley or watercress, and lemon wedges. Arrange a row of poached shrimps down the center of the fish. To cook shrimps: Place ¼ pound shrimps in a 1-quart microwave casserole, cover, and cook on High for 1 to 3 minutes until pink.

Serve as a first course on a buffet table, or as a light lunch with salad, bread, wine, and dessert.

TIPS   Before buying fish, make sure it will fit on your cooking dish and in your oven.

The eye is covered with aluminum foil to reflect microwave energy and keep it from cooking. If foil is wrapped smoothly under the fish the foil will not arc.

A large whole fish poaches more evenly on Medium power than on High.

Gamberetti all'Aglio
SHRIMPS WITH GARLIC

Servings: 4   Cooking time: 7 to 10 minutes

2 tablespoons butter
2 tablespoons olive oil
3 garlic cloves, minced
1½ pounds medium-size
   shrimps, shelled and deveined

2 tablespoons chopped fresh
   parsley
Lemon wedges

In a 9-inch round or 8-inch-square microwave dish, combine butter, oil, and garlic. Cook on High for 1 to 1½ minutes, until garlic is tender but not brown.

Stir in shrimps to coat, then spread them out evenly in a single layer. Cover with vented plastic wrap and cook on High for 3 minutes. Stir, moving shrimps from the outside edges to the inside. Re-cover and cook for 4 to 7 minutes more, until shrimps turn pink and opaque, stirring every 2 minutes. Allow to stand, covered, for 1 to 2 minutes.

Stir well before serving in individual bowls with sauce. Sprinkle with parsley and serve lemon wedges.

Wine Selection: Ciro' Bianco

SERVING SUGGESTIONS   Begin with Gnocchi di Patate sauced with Salsa di Pomodoro II (see Index for pages). Serve shrimps with crusty Italian bread and a salad.

Conchiglie con Pignoli
SCALLOPS WITH PINE NUTS

Servings: 4   Cooking time: 5 to 8 minutes

1 pound scallops
2 tablespoons olive oil
2 garlic cloves, minced
¼ cup dry bread crumbs
¼ cup pignoli (pine nuts)
¼ teaspoon salt

⅛ teaspoon freshly ground
   pepper, or to taste
2 tablespoons chopped fresh
   parsley
Lemon wedges

In a 9-inch round or 8-inch-square microwave dish, spread scallops in a single layer. Cover with vented plastic wrap. Cook on High for 3 to 5 minutes, until scallops are opaque and the centers flake, stirring to reposition scallops halfway through cooking. Divide cooked scallops among 4 ramekins.

In a small microwaveproof mixing bowl, combine oil and garlic. Cook on High for 30 to 45 seconds, until garlic is tender but not brown. Stir in remaining ingredients except lemon wedges. Spoon mixture over scallops.

Place ramekins in a circular pattern on the oven shelf, allowing 1-inch space between them. Cook on High for 1 to 2 minutes until heated through, repositioning halfway through cooking.

Wine Selection: Northern Italian Chardonnay

SERVING SUGGESTIONS   Begin with Risotto or Carciofi Ripieni, Stuffed Artichokes (see Index for pages).

Calamari Ripieni
STUFFED SQUID

The sack body of the squid is perfect for stuffing. We first tasted stuffed squid in an Italian restaurant in New York. After numerous journeys to the restaurant we improvised this version.

Servings: 4   **Cooking time: 25 to 30 minutes**

*1½ pounds dressed squids with
    tentacles
3 tablespoons olive oil
3 garlic cloves, minced
1 cup fine dry bread crumbs
¼ cup grated Parmesan cheese
6 tablespoons chopped fresh
    parsley
1 egg, beaten*

*Freshly ground pepper, about ¼
    teaspoon
2 cups peeled and chopped ripe
    tomatoes, preferably plum, or
    undrained canned, chopped
1 tablespoon chopped fresh basil,
    or ½ teaspoon crushed dried
½ teaspoon salt (less if using
    frozen squids)*

Rinse squids well and check to see that there is no remaining cartilage. Dry. Remove tentacles and discard or, if desired, add to sauce when stuffed squids are added.

In a medium-size microwaveproof bowl, combine 1 tablespoon oil and 1 garlic clove. Cook on High for 30 to 45 seconds, until garlic is tender but not brown. Add bread crumbs, grated cheese, 2 tablespoons parsley, the egg, and about ⅛ teaspoon pepper. Mix well and set aside for stuffing.

Prepare poaching sauce by combining remaining 2 tablespoons oil and 2 garlic cloves in a 3-quart microwave casserole with lid. Cook on High for 45 seconds to 1 minute, until garlic is tender but not brown. Stir in remaining 4 tablespoons parsley, the tomatoes, basil, salt, and remaining ⅛ teaspoon pepper. Cook on High for 10 minutes, stirring once or twice.

Meanwhile, stuff each squid until approximately two thirds full; slit opening slightly if necessary. Place stuffed squids in heated sauce, with the wider sections toward the outside rim of the casserole. Add tentacles at this point, if desired. Cover and cook on *Medium* (50% power) for 12 to 18 minutes, or until squids are tender and have turned opaque, gently turning them over and repositioning them after 6 minutes. The cooked stuffing will cause the squids to puff out like little eggs. Allow to stand covered for 3 to 5 minutes before serving.

Serve with poaching juices over plain spaghetti. Garnish with additional parsley.

Wine Selection: Barbera d'Alba or Verdicchio Classico

TIPS   To dress your own squids, follow directions in Zuppa di Frutta di Mare (see Index).

Overstuffing a squid will cause stuffing to seep out.

Calamari al Nino
NINO'S SQUID

This dish is named for an Italian man from Calabria. He didn't actually concoct it although, like most Italian men, he appreciates good food. The combination of ingredients rather reminded us of him. But is it the fiery pepper, or the slippery squid? There are some things that are better left unsaid.

Servings: 4   Cooking time: about 20 minutes

2 tablespoons olive oil
2 garlic cloves, minced
2 cups peeled and chopped ripe
   tomatoes, preferably plum, or
   undrained canned, chopped
¼ cup finely chopped fresh
   parsley
2 tablespoons chopped fresh
   basil, or 1 teaspoon crushed
   dried

½ teaspoon hot pepper flakes
½ teaspoon salt (less if using
   frozen squids)
¼ teaspoon freshly ground
   pepper
1½ pounds dressed squids with
   tentacles

In a 3-quart casserole, combine oil and garlic. Cook on High for 30 to 45 seconds, until garlic is tender but not brown. Add remaining ingredients except squids, stirring to blend. Cook on High for 10 minutes, stirring once or twice.

Meanwhile, rinse squids well. Cut each squid crosswise, into ¼-inch rounds. Discard tentacles, or slice them and add to sauce. Add squid rounds to sauce; stir. Cook on High for 8 to 12 minutes, or until squids are tender and have turned opaque, stirring after 4 minutes.

Serve over plain spaghetti, with crusty bread and a salad.

Wine Selection: Ciro' Rosso or Corvo Salaparuta

TIPS   Because these squids are not stuffed they can be cooked on High power.

They are cooked uncovered to prevent the sauce from becoming watery.

8
Pollame e Carne
Poultry and Meats

Shopping for meats in a small northern Italian town is quite different from meat shopping in this country, and it is the clientele and the merchandise that make it so. The local *macelleria* is no respecter of classes when it comes to the search for freshness. It is not unusual to see a well-groomed woman in a tailored, cashmere coat waiting her turn beside a grandmother in a black, misbuttoned sweater and scarf.

In one particular market, there were other characters that caught our attention. Poking their snouts out at us through the open storefront were three enormous pigs, heads only, who unlike the ones in the fairy tale had not escaped their captor. Their brows were wreathed in crowns of bay leaves, and beneath their jowls hung necklaces of pink and beige sausages. The impish grins frozen on their faces indicated that they were privy to a secret we would never know. Beside this trio, and above the archway to the *macelleria*, the owner had carefully strung ham legs in a row that kicked in the breeze like a Radio City chorus line. There was no question that the merchandise was fresh. In fact, we even had visions of taking our meat home on a leash.

Color page one: Ossobuco on Risotto alla Milanese (Veal Shanks Simmered in Sauce on Saffron Rice) with Cipolline in Agrodolce (Sweet and Sour Green Onions)

Color page two: Lasagne al Ragu (Lasagna with Sausage-Meat Sauce and Ricotta Cheese), back; Lasagne Verde (Green Lasagna with Meat and White Sauces), front.

Color page three: (Clockwise from left rear) Cassata Ricotta (Sicilian Ricotta Cake), Crostata di Frutta Fresca (Fresh Fruit Tart), Zuppa Inglese (Italian Rum Custard Cake), Torta di Mandorle e Pignoli (Almond and Pine Nut Cake)

Color page four: Baci di Amori (Chocolate Truffles), Gelato di Amaretto con Croccante (Amaretto Ice Cream with sprinklings of caramelized almond brittle), Granita di Limone (Lemon Ice), molded and served with candied violets

Of all the meats, veal is the most popular in Italy, and is less expensive to buy there than in this country. The cut and quality differ and it would be safe to say that both are better in Italy. This is one reason we have limited our use of veal to veal roasts and shanks, and eliminated veal cutlet in favor of a chicken cutlet.

When less expensive cuts of veal are simmered in a presoaked clay simmerpot, the cook can achieve the same slow-cooked flavor found via Italian pan-roasting, but in much less time. Ossobuco is a perfect example. Here veal shanks are simmered with tomatoes, vegetables, beef stock, herbs, and wine. When served on a platter with a Risotto alla Milanese, the dish is elevated to that superb quality usually reserved for royalty.

When it comes to braising beef roasts, the microwave and clay simmerpot are an unbeatable combination. Clay or terracotta casseroles are often favored for conventional braising, but a disadvantage is that they are not suitable for reheating. Not so with the microwave where the precooked or leftover meat can be reheated right in the pot. The long, slow cooking that is part of simmerpot cooking will cause the meat to brown gradually. So for a perfectly sumptuous Manzo al Barolo, Beef Braised in Red Wine, zesty Manzo al Espresso, Beef Braised in Espresso Coffee Gravy, or succulent Arrosto di Agnello, Roast Lamb, the clay simmerpot is an excellent investment.

Pork makes an appearance in an impressive Arrosto di Maiale di Capodimonte, a pork loin rolled around prosciutto, mozzarella, and Italian olives. For everyday eating, good Italian pork sausage is complemented by sweet green peppers in Salsiccie e Peperoni. How do you find good-quality sausage? One way is to make it yourself with the basic hot or sweet sausage recipe in this chapter.

We have substituted flattened chicken breast or cutlets for veal cutlets. The flavor and appearance are surprisingly similar, and we feel that the cooking control is better with a slightly thicker, more succulent chicken breast than with a thinner piece of veal. The chicken cutlets can be quickly cooked on High power for the Milanese, Marsala, and Piccata styles, to name a few.

Mixed chicken pieces are whisked into the well-known Pollo alla Cacciatora, and Cornish game hens are cooked in a tasty gin-spiked sauce for Pollastrino al Gin.

This is the chapter to show you that although meat is not necessarily served daily in the home, Italians show their artistry in a vast repertoire with poultry and meat dishes. We think that you will be delighted with the selections in this chapter.

Petti di Pollo alla Milanese
BREADED CHICKEN CUTLET IN THE MILAN STYLE

Petti di pollo are chicken breasts that are pounded, dipped into beaten egg and bread crumbs, then fried in hot oil. It is the hot oil that adds flavor and gives the even brown color. We have used the oil and butter in the coating to accomplish the same purpose in the microwave. The method is clean and easy; the chicken stays moist and juicy.

This basic recipe can be embellished to produce the many cutlet recipes that are so popular in Italian cooking.

Servings: 4   **Cooking time: 10 to 15 minutes**

2 whole chicken breasts, about 2
   pounds, halved, skinned, and
   boned
2 tablespoons butter
1 tablespoon vegetable oil
1 egg, beaten
¾ cup fine dry unflavored bread
   crumbs

¼ cup grated Parmesan cheese
¼ teaspoon salt
⅛ teaspoon freshly ground
   pepper
Lemon wedges

Place chicken between 2 pieces of wax paper and flatten with a meat pounder to about ¼-inch thickness.

Place butter in a medium-size microwaveproof bowl or glass pie plate. Cook on High for 45 seconds to 1 minute, until melted. Stir in oil and egg until completely blended.

In a separate plate or on wax paper, combine bread crumbs, cheese, salt, and pepper.

Dip each piece of chicken into the butter-egg mixture and then into the crumb mixture, pressing coating into place with hands.

Arrange chicken pieces with thicker sections toward the outside in a 2-quart microwave dish (12 x 8 inches). Cook on High for 6 minutes. Turn over and reposition chicken pieces to allow thicker portions to cook more evenly; rotate dish ½ turn. Cook on High for 4 to 7 minutes more, or until meat tests done. Allow to stand for 2 to 5 minutes before serving.

Serve with lemon wedges.
Wine Selection: Pinot Bianco

VARIATIONS   For Petti di Pollo alla Noci, Chicken with Nuts, substitute 1 cup finely chopped walnuts for bread crumbs and cheese. Follow basic recipe instructions. If desired, this variation can be served with Pesto, Uncooked Basil Sauce (see Index). After cooking the cutlets, spread the top of each one with a thin layer of pesto. During standing time the pesto will melt into the nut coating. Chicken with pesto can be served hot or chilled.

SERVING SUGGESTIONS   Begin with Fettuccine Alfredo or Risotto or Maccheroni al Vodka (see Index for pages).

TIP   Cooking cutlets uncovered will give them a drier exterior.

Petti di Pollo alla Marsala
BREADED CHICKEN CUTLETS WITH MARSALA

The spark of Marsala catapults these chicken cutlets to a superb company dish. It is very continental and very light.

Servings: 4   Cooking time: 15 to 20 minutes

Petti di Pollo alla Milanese   *¼ cup thinly sliced scallions*
   (preceding recipe)   *½ cup Marsala wine*
2 tablespoons butter

Prepare Petti di Pollo alla Milanese. After cooking, remove chicken cutlets to another dish.
   Add butter and scallions to cooking dish. Cook on High for 1 to 1½ minutes, stirring halfway through cooking. Stir in wine and continue to cook for 3 minutes, stirring once.
   Return chicken to the dish with the wine sauce. Cover with wax paper and cook on High for 2 to 5 minutes, or until heated through, rotating dish once or twice. Serve immediately.
   Serve cutlets with sauce spooned over and lemon wedges.
   Wine Selection: Northern Italian Chardonnay

VARIATIONS   Substitute Petti di Pollo alla Noci, a variation of Petti di Pollo alla Milanese.
   For Petti di Pollo con i Funghi, Chicken Cutlets with Mushrooms, prepare and cook Petti di Pollo alla Milanese. Remove chicken from

dish to serving platter and cover loosely with foil to keep warm. Follow basic recipe, adding ¼ pound thin-sliced mushrooms to cooking dish along with wine. Cook on High for 3 to 4 minutes, until mushrooms are tender, stirring once.

Pour sauce over cutlets and serve.

SERVING SUGGESTIONS   Begin with Fettuccine alla Gorgonzola or Risi e Bisi, Rice and Pea Soup (see Index for pages).

Petti di Pollo alla Parmigiana
BREADED CHICKEN CUTLETS WITH CHEESE AND TOMATO SAUCE

Servings: 4   Preparation time: 15 to 20 minutes
                                                without tomato
                                                sauce

Petti di Pollo alla Milanese (see   *Salsa di Pomodoro III (see Index)*
  Index)   *or prepared tomato sauce*
8 ounces mozzarella cheese,
  sliced thin

Prepare Petti di Pollo alla Milanese. After cooking, top each cutlet with sliced cheese (reserving 4 slices) and pour sauce over all. Cover with wax paper and cook on Medium (50% power) for 5 to 10 minutes, or until sauce is heated through. Top with reserved cheese and cook, uncovered, 1 minute more.

Wine Selection: Sangiovese di Romagna

TIP   Cheese is cooked on Medium to prevent it from becoming tough and rubbery. Wax paper helps to heat the cheese evenly without adding excess moisture.

Petti di Pollo con Castagne
BREADED CHICKEN CUTLETS WITH CHESTNUT STUFFING

When turkeys were brought from the New World, the Italians took to them with gusto to produce a *tacchino arrosto ripieno con castagne*, roast turkey stuffed with chestnuts. We have taken this idea and made a chestnut stuffing for chicken cutlets.

Servings: 4   Cooking time: about 30 minutes

¼ *pound whole chestnuts in the*
shells
1 *cup chicken stock*
2 *whole chicken breasts, about 2*
pounds, halved, skinned, and
boned
2 *tablespoons butter*
2 *eggs*
1 *tablespoon vegetable oil*
¾ *cup fine dry unflavored bread*
crumbs

¼ *cup grated Parmesan cheese*
¼ *teaspoon salt*
⅛ *teaspoon freshly ground*
pepper
½ *cup raisins*
1 *apple, peeled and chopped*
1 *cup coarse fresh bread crumbs*
2 *tablespoons chopped fresh*
parsley
1 *sage leaf, chopped, or* ⅛
teaspoon powdered

On the round side of each chestnut shell, use a sharp knife to make 2 slits that cross in an X. Arrange chestnuts, slit side up, in a circle around the outer edge of a 9-inch glass or microwave cake dish. Cook on High for 2 to 4 minutes, until steam forces the shells to curl back.

Peel off the shells and place the chestnuts into a 1-quart microwave casserole with the chicken stock. Cover and cook on High for 10 to 15 minutes, stirring once or twice.

Meanwhile prepare chicken. Place chicken cutlets between 2 pieces of wax paper and flatten with a meat pounder to about ¼-inch thickness.

Place butter in a medium-size microwaveproof bowl or glass pie plate. Cook on High for 45 seconds to 1 minute, until melted. In a separate bowl, beat 1 egg. Stir beaten egg and oil into butter until completely blended. In a separate plate or on wax paper, combine ¾ cup fine bread crumbs, the cheese, salt, and pepper.

Dip each piece of chicken into the butter-egg mixture and then into the crumb mixture, pressing coating into place with hands. Set cutlets aside in a single layer on a piece of wax paper.

With a slotted spoon remove cooked chestnuts from oven and reserve 4 whole chestnuts. Chop the remainder of the chestnuts, and reserve ½ cup chicken stock for stuffing.

To make stuffing: Beat remaining egg in a small mixing bowl. Add chopped chestnuts, ½ cup chicken stock, and remaining ingredients.

Form chestnut stuffing into 4 mounds and arrange in a 2-quart microwave dish (12 x 8 inches) leaving the center of the dish open.

Cover each mound with a breaded chicken cutlet. Cook on High for 10 to 13 minutes, rotating dish ½ turn halfway through cooking. Allow to stand 2 to 5 minutes before serving. To serve, top each cutlet with a reserved whole chestnut.

Wine Selection: Tocai Friulano

TIP   The center of the dish is kept open to allow for more even cooking.

SERVING SUGGESTIONS   Begin with Fettuccine Alfredo or Zuppa di Scarola e Polpettine, Escarole and Meatball Soup (see Index for pages).

Piccata di Petti di Pollo
CHICKEN CUTLETS WITH LEMON

Unlike the other cutlets in this chapter, this recipe calls for a light flour coating rather than oil and breading. Because of this, we cook them on the browning dish which will brown the cutlets through surface heat.

Servings: 4   **Cooking time: 4 minutes**

2 whole chicken breasts, about 2
   pounds, halved, skinned, and
   boned
¼ cup flour
¼ teaspoon salt
⅛ teaspoon freshly ground
   pepper

3 tablespoons butter
2 tablespoons lemon juice
1 lemon, sliced thin
2 tablespoons chopped fresh
   parsley

Place chicken between 2 pieces of wax paper and flatten with a meat pounder to about ¼-inch thickness.

In a pie plate, combine flour, salt, and pepper. Coat cutlets with flour mixture and set aside.

Place a microwave browning dish in oven and preheat according to manufacturer's instructions for chicken, for 6 to 8 minutes on High. Place butter on the heated dish and spread to coat the surface.

Add cutlets, pressing them down with a metal spatula to make good surface contact. Cook on High for 2 minutes. Turn over and press down again. Cook for 2 minutes more, or until done.

Transfer cooked chicken to a serving platter. Add lemon juice to browning dish and stir with fork. Cook on High for 1 to 2 minutes to deglaze dish. Pour deglazing over chicken and serve topped with lemon slices and chopped parsley.

Wine Selection: Soave

SERVING SUGGESTIONS   Begin with Fonduta, Cheese Fondue, or Cappelle di Funghi Ripieni, Stuffed Mushroom Caps, or Fettuccine alla Carbonara (see Index for pages).

Involtini di Pollo con Prosciutto e Formaggio

CHICKEN BREASTS ROLLED WITH PROSCIUTTO AND CHEESE

Rolled with Fontina cheese from Valle d'Aosta and simmered in cream and white wine, these chicken *involtini*, or little rolls, display a Swiss character. Fresh sage adds so much to this dish, that it would be a shame not to scout around for some before making it. Grow your own, for it is hearty and in many locales will last through the winter.

Servings: 4 to 6   **Cooking time: 10 minutes**

6 boneless chicken cutlets, about
  1½ pounds altogether, or 3
  small whole chicken breasts,
  halved, skinned, and boned
6 slices of prosciutto, about ¼
  pound
6 slices of Fontina cheese, 2
  ounces

3 fresh sage leaves, or ⅛
  teaspoon powdered
2 tablespoons butter
1 medium-size onion, chopped
1 tablespoon flour
¼ cup chicken stock
¼ cup dry white wine
2 tablespoons heavy cream

Between 2 pieces of wax paper, flatten chicken pieces with a meat pounder to between ¼- and ½-inch thickness.

Place 1 slice of prosciutto, 1 slice of cheese, and ½ sage leaf or a pinch of powdered sage on each chicken breast. Roll up each breast and fasten with a toothpick.

In a 2-quart microwave casserole, combine butter and onion and cook on High for 2 minutes, or until onion is slightly tender. Stir in flour to blend. Stir in chicken stock and white wine. Place chicken breasts, seam side down, in the casserole and cover with wax paper. Cook on High for 6 minutes, turning over and repositioning halfway through cooking.

Stir in heavy cream. Re-cover and cook on High for 1 to 2 minutes, or until sauce bubbles. Allow to stand, covered, for 5 minutes before serving.

Wine Selection: Gavi

SERVING SUGGESTIONS   Serve with a side dish of Cipolline in Agrodolce, Sweet and Sour Green Onions, or Zucchini Rapido, Quick Zucchini (see Index for pages).

Pollo alla Cacciatora
HUNTER-STYLE CHICKEN

It seems that more than one culture has a chicken dish called "hunter-style." The bright red sauce and stripes of green pepper always reminded us of a hunter's flannel shirt against a forest thicket. *Cacciatora* is used here to mean hunter-style, but the noun *cacciatora* also means hunter's jacket. In Italian there is no doubt a world of difference between the two usages, but it is close enough to satisfy our imagination.

Servings: 4   Cooking time: 35 minutes

1 tablespoon olive oil
1 medium-size onion, sliced
1 garlic clove, minced
1 medium-size green pepper,
*   stem and seeds removed, cut*
*   into ¼-inch strips*
¼ cup tomato paste
½ pound fresh mushrooms,
*   sliced thin*
1 cup peeled and chopped ripe
*   tomatoes, preferably plum, or*
*   undrained canned, chopped*

¼ cup dry white wine
1 tablespoon chopped fresh basil,
*   or 1 teaspoon crushed dried*
¼ teaspoon salt
⅛ teaspoon freshly ground
*   pepper*
2½- to 3-pound chicken, cut into
*   serving pieces*

Soak a 3-quart clay simmerpot in cold water for 15 minutes. Combine oil, onion, garlic, and green pepper in simmerpot or a microwave casserole with lid. Cover and cook on High for 2 to 3 minutes, or until vegetables are tender. Stir in tomato paste. Add remaining ingredients except chicken; stir.

Place chicken pieces, skin side down, in the casserole, with thicker pieces to the outside. Cover and cook on High for 10 minutes. Turn chicken over and reposition pieces to allow thicker portions to cook more evenly. Re-cover and cook on *Medium* (50% power) for 20 to 25 minutes, or until tender.

Allow to stand for 5 minutes. Serve with Polenta (see Index).
Wine Selection: Barbera

Pollastrino al Gin
CORNISH HENS SIMMERED IN GIN SAUCE

Juniper berries are sometimes combined with squab or pheasant in northern Italian cooking. For convenience and availability in this country, we have substituted Cornish hens and gin, a juniper-flavored liquor.

During cooking the gin mellows and brings out the sweetness of the onion. The result is a delicate rosy sauce that lightly coats the juicy hens.

Servings: 4   Cooking time: 40 to 45 minutes

2 slices of pancetta or bacon, cut
   into ½-inch cubes
2 garlic cloves, minced
1 medium-size onion, chopped
   fine
1 tablespoon tomato paste

1 teaspoon grated lemon rind
¼ cup gin
¼ cup chicken stock
2 Cornish game hens, 1¾ to 2
   pounds each, split lengthwise

Soak a 3-quart clay simmerpot in cold water for 15 minutes. Combine pancetta, garlic, and onion in the simmerpot or a microwave casserole with lid. Cover and cook on High for 2 to 3 minutes, or until vegetables are tender. Stir in tomato paste, lemon rind, gin, and stock.

Place hens, skin side down, in the sauce. Cover and cook on High for 5 minutes. Turn hens over and rearrange to allow thicker portions to cook more evenly.

Cover and cook on *Medium* (50% power) for 25 to 30 minutes, or until meat tests done. Remove hens to serving platter and cover with foil.

Cook remaining juices, uncovered, on High for 5 minutes to reduce; skim off fat. Serve hens and juices over Polenta Formaggio, Cheese Polenta (see Index).

Wine Selection: Sauvignon Bianco

TIPS   We have called for the larger hens that will serve 4 when halved. If you can not find the larger hens, buy those as close as possible to the size indicated and scale down your cooking time slightly. Compensate for the smaller portion of meat with a first course (see Serving Suggestions), or serve hens with Italian sausage over polenta.

If a browner appearance is desired for the chicken, we recommend complementing microwave cooking with the conventional method. While pancetta, onion, and garlic are cooking in the microwave, lightly brown fleshy sides of hens in 2 tablespoons of hot oil in a large skillet; drain hens and add to casserole.

Arrosto di Vitello
ROAST VEAL WITH ROSEMARY AND WHITE WINE

Servings: 6   Cooking time: about 1 hour

3-pound veal roast, flattened, or   ½ teaspoon crushed
   a rolled roast   peppercorns
2 garlic cloves, minced   3 tablespoons butter
2 sprigs of fresh rosemary, or 2   ½ cup dry white wine
   teaspoons crushed dried   2 tablespoons flour
½ teaspoon salt   ¼ cup chopped fresh parsley

Soak a 3-quart clay simmerpot in cold water for 15 minutes.

If veal is a flat roast, sprinkle one side with garlic, rosemary, salt, and pepper. Roll tightly and secure in several places with string. If veal is a rolled roast, pierce outside with a small sharp knife and insert garlic and rosemary in the slits, positioning the slits so that the surface is stuffed at even intervals. Sprinkle the outside with salt and pepper.

Place butter in the soaked simmerpot, or in a microwave casserole with lid. Cook on High for 30 seconds to 1 minute, to melt butter. Add meat, fat side down. Pour in wine. Cover and cook on High for 15 minutes.

Turn meat over, rotate dish ⅓ turn, and re-cover. Cook on *Medium* (50% power) for 40 minutes, turning over and basting halfway through cooking. Rotate dish 2 or 3 times during cooking. Test meat for doneness; a meat thermometer should register 165°F.

If more cooking is necessary, cover and continue to cook on Medium for 10 to 20 minutes more, or until veal is done.

Transfer veal from casserole to a serving platter and cover with foil to keep warm.

In a small custard cup or bowl, combine flour with 3 tablespoons meat drippings; stir to make a smooth paste. Stir paste into remaining drippings. Cook, uncovered, on *High* for 3 to 6 minutes, or until gravy comes to a boil and thickens slightly, stirring occasionally.

To serve: Carve veal into ¼-inch slices and spoon gravy over each piece. Sprinkle with parsley.

Wine Selection: Fiano di Avellino

TIP   The internal temperature of the meat will rise 10° to 15°F during standing time. Serving temperature should be 175°F.

Ossobuco
VEAL SHANKS SIMMERED IN SAUCE

This is the classic veal dish from Milan that is best when served with a creamy Risotto. Veal shanks still attached to bone and rich marrow, hardly seem the basis for one of the most famous of Italian dishes. Yet when the veal is cooked to fork tender doneness in a velvety tomato-beef sauce it deserves nothing less than royal treatment in its presentation.

Servings: 4   **Cooking time: 1 to 1¼ hours**

1 tablespoon olive oil
1 garlic clove, crushed
1 medium-size onion, chopped
   fine
1 carrot, chopped fine
1 celery rib, chopped fine
2 tablespoons flour
1 cup peeled, seeded, and
   chopped ripe tomatoes,
   preferably plum, or undrained
   canned, chopped

½ cup beef stock
¼ cup dry white wine
2 tablespoons chopped fresh
   parsley
1 teaspoon grated lemon rind
¼ teaspoon salt
¼ teaspoon freshly ground
   pepper
4 veal shanks with bone, 2 to 2½
   pounds, cut into 2-inch-thick
   pieces, both meat and bone

Soak a 3-quart clay simmerpot in cold water for 15 minutes. In the soaked simmerpot, or a microwave casserole with lid, combine oil, garlic, onion, carrot, and celery. Cover and cook on High for 3 minutes, or until vegetables are slightly tender, stirring once.

Blend in flour. Add remaining ingredients except veal; stir well. Arrange veal shanks on top. Cover and cook on High for 15 minutes; stir sauce and reposition shanks, moving the less-cooked ones to the outside.

Re-cover and cook on *Medium* (50% power) for 40 to 60 minutes, or until tender, repositioning and stirring halfway through cooking. Allow to stand, covered, for 10 minutes before serving.

Wine Selection: Barbera

Arrosto di Vitello e Funghi
ROAST VEAL WITH MUSHROOM GRAVY

Servings: 6 to 8   **Cooking time: about 1 hour**

3- to 3½-pound rolled veal roast
½ teaspoon salt
¼ teaspoon freshly ground
  pepper
3 tablespoons butter
1 medium-size onion, chopped
  fine
1 celery rib, chopped fine
1 medium-size carrot, peeled
  and chopped fine

2 tablespoons flour
1 sprig of fresh rosemary, or ½
  teaspoon crushed dried
½ cup dry white wine
1 pound fresh mushrooms, sliced
  thin
¼ cup finely chopped fresh
  parsley

Soak a 3-quart simmerpot in cold water for 15 minutes. Rub outside of roast with salt and pepper.

In the soaked simmerpot, or in a microwave casserole with lid, combine butter, onion, celery, and carrot. Cover and cook on High for 3 minutes, or until vegetables are slightly tender, stirring once. Sprinkle vegetables with flour and stir until liquid has absorbed flour to form a smooth paste. Add rosemary and wine; stir.

Place veal in the casserole. Cover and cook on High for 15 minutes, rotating once. Turn meat over and baste. Re-cover and cook on *Medium* (50% power) for 45 to 50 minutes, or until veal is tender and a meat thermometer registers 165°F, turning meat over and basting halfway through cooking. Rotate dish 2 to 3 times during cooking.

Transfer meat to a serving platter and cover with foil. Allow to stand for 10 to 15 minutes.

Meanwhile, strain the cooking juices, forcing vegetables through strainer. Return strained juices and vegetables to the casserole. Cook uncovered on High for 4 to 6 minutes until boiling, stirring once. Add mushrooms; stir. Continue to cook for 3 or 4 minutes more, stirring once halfway through cooking. Stir in parsley.

To serve: Slice roast and spoon mushroom gravy over slices.
Wine Selection: Pinot Grigio

Vitello Tonnato
COLD ROAST VEAL IN TUNA SAUCE

An unusual flavor combination of veal and tuna, this dish originally hails from the area around Milan. It is lovely for a buffet table for its ease of serving and exquisite presentation.

Servings: 6 to 8   **Cooking time: about 1 hour**

Arrosto di Vitello e Funghi, Roast Veal with Mushroom Gravy (preceding recipe)*
1 can (7 ounces) Italian tuna fish packed in olive oil
4 flat anchovy fillets
3 tablespoons capers

¼ cup lemon juice
1 cup olive oil
1 cup Maionese (see Index) or prepared mayonnaise
2 lemons, sliced thin, as garnish
Fresh parsley, as garnish
Additional capers, as garnish

Right before serving, in the bowl of a food processor or blender, combine tuna, anchovies, capers, lemon juice, and oil; process into a creamy paste. Fold mixture into mayonnaise. Spread a serving platter with ½ cup of this tuna sauce.

Carve veal into thin slices and arrange slices to overlap slightly on the serving platter spread with sauce. Cover smoothly with remaining sauce. Garnish with lemon slices, parsley, and additional capers.
Wine Selection: To'cai Friulano

SERVING SUGGESTIONS   For a sit-down meal, begin with Risi e Bisi, Rice and Pea Soup (see Index) and follow with a green salad.

*Follow basic veal roast recipe, but eliminate flour and mushrooms. After roast has finished cooking, remove it from dish and refrigerate for 3 to 4 hours. Discard vegetables and juices, or freeze them for later use in soup or gravy.

Spezzatino di Vitello con i Peperoni
VEAL STEW WITH PEPPERS

Spezzatino is the Italian word for stew, one most commonly made with veal and any variety of vegetables.

Servings: 4 to 6   Cooking time: 1¼ hours

1 tablespoon butter
1 medium-size onion, chopped
fine
2 tablespoons tomato paste
1 cup peeled and chopped ripe
tomatoes, preferably plum, or
undrained canned, chopped
¼ teaspoon crushed dried thyme
1 tablespoon chopped fresh basil,
or 1 teaspoon crushed dried

1 teaspoon salt
¼ teaspoon freshly ground
pepper
¼ teaspoon red pepper flakes
(optional)
1½ to 2 pounds boneless veal
stew meat, shoulder or shank,
cut into 1-inch cubes
4 large green peppers, cut
lengthwise into ¼-inch strips

Soak a 3-quart clay simmerpot in cold water for 15 minutes. In the soaked simmerpot, or in a casserole with lid, combine butter and onion. Cover and cook on High for 1 to 2 minutes, or until onion is slightly tender. Stir in tomato paste.

Add remaining ingredients except green peppers; stir well. Cover and cook on High for 15 minutes, stirring twice. Re-cover and cook on *Medium* (50% power) for 50 minutes, stirring twice.

Add peppers. Cover and cook on Medium for 10 to 15 minutes, or until peppers and meat are tender. Allow to stand, covered, for 5 minutes before serving.

Wine Selection: Ciro' Rosso

SERVING SUGGESTIONS   Begin with Spaghetti all'Aglio e Olio, Spaghetti with Garlic and Oil (see Index). Serve with a green salad and bread.

Polpettone
MEAT LOAF

This meat loaf made with veal has a delicate flavor. It is cooked in wine and topped with cheese, and may be served cold as an antipasto.

Servings: 6   Cooking time: 30 to 45 minutes

2 pounds ground veal
1 cup fine dry bread crumbs
1 medium-size onion, chopped
   fine
2 eggs, beaten
½ teaspoon freshly grated
   nutmeg

½ teaspoon salt
¼ cup grated Parmesan cheese
¼ cup dry white wine
4 ounces mozzarella cheese,
   sliced thin

In a mixing bowl, combine all ingredients except wine and cheese. Shape into a loaf 9 by 5 inches. Place in a 2-quart microwave dish (12 x 8 inches). Pour wine over the loaf. Cook on High for 5 minutes. Cook on *Medium* (50% power) for 25 to 35 minutes, or until loaf tests done and a meat thermometer registers 165°F.

Cover the top of loaf with a single layer of cheese. Allow to stand for 5 to 10 minutes; in this time the cheese should melt. If cheese has not melted, cook on Medium for 1 to 3 minutes to melt.

Serve plain or with Salsa di Pomodoro I, Tomato Sauce I (see Index).
Wine Selection: Chianti Classico Riserva

SERVING SUGGESTIONS   Serve with Patate al Rosmarino, Potatoes with Rosemary (see Index).

Manzo al Barolo
BEEF BRAISED IN RED WINE

Barolo wine comes from northwestern Piedmont where Nebbiolo grapes are grown. For that reason we affectionately call this concoction our Piedmont Pot Roast.

Servings: 6 to 8   **Cooking time: 1¼ hours**

1 tablespoon olive oil
2 garlic cloves, minced
1 medium-size onion, chopped
   fine
1 medium-size carrot, peeled
   and chopped fine
1 celery rib, chopped fine
3 tablespoons tomato paste
1 bay leaf

⅛ teaspoon crushed dried thyme
½ cup dry red wine
½ cup beef stock
½ teaspoon salt
¼ teaspoon freshly ground
   pepper
3 to 3½ pounds rolled bottom
   round or rump roast

Soak a 3-quart clay simmerpot in cold water for 15 minutes. In the soaked simmerpot, or in a microwave casserole with lid, combine oil, garlic, onion, carrot, and celery. Cover and cook on High for 2 to 3 minutes, or until vegetables are slightly tender, stirring once. Add 2 tablespoons tomato paste; stir. Stir in remaining ingredients except meat and 1 tablespoon tomato paste.

Place roast in casserole, fat side up. Cover and cook on High for 15 minutes, rotating dish once. Turn meat over and baste. Re-cover and cook on *Medium* (50% power) for 60 to 70 minutes, until meat is tender, turning it over and basting halfway through cooking. Rotate dish 2 or 3 times during cooking.

Transfer meat to a serving platter and cover with foil. Allow to stand for 10 to 15 minutes.

Meanwhile, skim off as much fat as possible from the cookindg juices. Stir in remaining 1 tablespoon tomato paste. Cook on High for 5 to 8 minutes, until sauce is thickened, stirring every 2 minutes. Slice meat and serve with sauce.

Wine Selection: Barolo

SERVING SUGGESTIONS   Serve with Pure di Patate, Mashed Potatoes (see Index).

Manzo al Espresso
BEEF BRAISED IN ESPRESSO COFFEE GRAVY

In addition to fresh espresso coffee, a handful of coffee beans are tossed in at the end of cooking just for fun. They can then be served in the gravy with the meat, to be chewed on for lingering flavor. The idea is reminiscent of the coffee beans served in the licorice liqueur, Sambuca. "Why not?" Everybody needs to be eccentric once in a while.

Servings: 6 to 8   **Cooking time: about 1½ hours**

1 tablespoon butter
1 medium-size onion, chopped
  fine
2 tablespoons flour
¼ cup dry red wine
½ cup prepared strong espresso
  coffee

½ teaspoon sugar
½ teaspoon salt
¼ teaspoon freshly ground
  pepper
3 to 3½ pounds beef rump roast
Handful of coffee beans (optional)

Soak a 3-quart clay simmerpot in cold water for 15 minutes. In the soaked simmerpot, or in a microwave casserole with lid, combine butter and onion. Cover and cook on High for 2 minutes, or until onion is slightly tender. Stir in flour to make a smooth paste. Stir in remaining ingredients except meat and coffee beans.

Place meat in casserole, fat side up. Cover and cook on High for 15 minutes, rotating dish once. Turn meat over and baste. Re-cover and cook on *Medium* (50% power) for 65 to 70 minutes, until meat is tender, turning it over and basting halfway through cooking. Rotate dish 2 or 3 times during cooking.

Transfer meat to a serving platter and cover with foil. Allow to stand for 10 minutes.

Meanwhile, skim off as much fat as possible from the cooking juices. Add coffee beans to juices. Cook on High for 3 to 5 minutes, until boiling. Serve thin-sliced meat with espresso gravy.

Wine selection: Barolo

SERVING SUGGESTIONS   Begin with a light antipasto like Caponata, Cold Eggplant Appetizer, and serve with Fagliolini al Pomodoro, Green Beans with Tomato and Garlic, or Cappelle di Funghi Impannato, Breaded Mushroom Caps (see Index for pages).

Involtini di Manzo
STUFFED ROLLED BEEF

Servings: 4   Cooking time: about 30 minutes

*1 pound round steak, cut into
    four ¼-inch-thick slices,
    each about 6 x 4 inches*
*4 thin slices of pancetta or
    bacon, cut into halves*
4 thin slices of smoked ham
¼ cup fine dry bread crumbs
1 egg, beaten
¼ cup grated Parmesan cheese

*2 tablespoons chopped fresh
    parsley*
½ teaspoon salt
*¼ teaspoon freshly ground
    pepper*
1 tablespoon olive oil
1 medium-size onion, chopped
2 tablespoons tomato paste
¼ cup dry red wine

On one side of each piece of beef, place 2 halves of pancetta. Top with a slice of ham, cut to fit.

In a small bowl, combine bread crumbs, egg, cheese, parsley, salt, and pepper. Spread on top of ham to within ½ inch of the edges. Starting with the longer side, roll each piece of meat and fasten with a toothpick.

In a 2-quart microwave casserole with lid, combine oil and onion.

Cover and cook on High for 1 to 1½ minutes, until onion is slightly tender. Stir in tomato paste, then wine.

Add meat rolls to casserole. Cover and cook on High for 5 minutes. Turn over rolls and reposition. Re-cover and cook on *Medium* (50% power) for 22 to 25 minutes or until tender, repositioning and basting halfway through cooking.

Transfer rolls to serving dish and cover.

Meanwhile, skim off as much fat as possible from cooking juices. Cook remaining juices on High for 2 to 5 minutes, until juices boil. Serve rolls with cooking juices spooned over them.

Wine Selection: Nebbiolo

SERVING SUGGESTIONS   Serve with Cappelle di Funghi Impannato, Breaded Mushroom Caps (see Index).

Arrosto di Agnello
ROAST LAMB

Servings: 6 to 8   Cooking time: 1¼ hours

3 to 3½ pounds lamb shank or   1 medium-size onion, chopped
   small leg of lamb   fine
½ teaspoon salt   1 sprig of fresh rosemary, or ½
¼ teaspoon freshly ground   teaspoon crushed dried
   pepper   2 teaspoons grated lemon rind
1 tablespoon butter   ¼ cup dry white wine
2 garlic cloves, minced

Soak a 3-quart clay simmerpot in cold water for 15 minutes. Rub outside of lamb with salt and pepper.

In the soaked simmerpot, or in a microwave casserole with lid, combine butter, garlic, and onion. Cover and cook on High for 1 to 1½ minutes, or until onion is slightly tender. Add rosemary, lemon rind, and wine; stir.

Add lamb. Cover and cook on High for 15 minutes, rotating dish once. Turn meat over and baste. Re-cover and cook on *Medium* (50% power) for 65 to 70 minutes, or until meat is tender and a meat thermometer registers 125°F (rare), turning meat over and basting halfway through cooking. Rotate dish 2 or 3 times throughout cooking.

Transfer lamb to a serving platter and cover with foil. Allow to stand for 10 to 15 minutes.

Meanwhile, skim off as much fat as possible from the cooking juices. Cook remaining juices on High for 3 to 5 minutes, until boiling. Slice meat and pour juices over slices.

Wine Selection: Chianti Classico Riserva or Greco di Tufo

TIP   The internal temperature of the lamb will rise 10° to 15°F during standing time.

SERVING SUGGESTIONS   Begin with pasta with Pesto, Uncooked Basil Sauce. Serve a side dish of Piselli con Prosciutto, Peas Sautéed with Prosciutto (see Index for pages).

Arrosto di Maiale di Capodimonte
STUFFED ROLLED PORK ROAST OF CAPODIMONTE

We like to call this roast our museum piece, and how it got that name is quite a story. One morning we were touring the Museo Nazionale di Capodimonte in Naples, which houses paintings by Lippi, Caravaggio, and Botticelli. At about 1:00 P.M., when we were ready to leave the museum, we found that we were locked in . . . all the guards had left for lunch, and in such a hurry that they had neglected to see if the visitors had left too! We were torn between spending the afternoon, unobserved, with a museum of art treasures, or attempting escape. We chose to scream from the second story that faced the front courtyard, and finally caught the attention of the last guard who was about to leave. Red-faced, he came back to let us out.

We pondered many times what particular food would cause these guards to forget all else in pursuit of it. After tasting this pork roast in a restaurant much later, we decided that it must have been something as seductive as this; it is sensational!

Servings: 6 to 8   **Cooking time: 1¼ hours**

3 pounds pork loin, cut
  lengthwise and butterflied
3 garlic cloves, minced
1 teaspoon salt
¼ teaspoon freshly ground
  pepper
¼ pound thin-sliced prosciutto
  or smoked ham
8 ounces mozzarella, sliced ⅛
  inch thick

24 imported black or purple
  olives, pitted
¼ cup pignoli (pine nuts)
1 teaspoon chopped fresh
  rosemary, or ¼ teaspoon
  crushed dried
¼ cup white wine

Have the pork pounded to ¾- to 1-inch thickness, making a rectangle 10 x 12 inches. Remove any excess outer fat from pork; freeze fat and save for sausage recipe (see Index). Rub both sides of meat with garlic, salt, and pepper.

Lay meat flat and arrange a single layer of prosciutto on one side. Top this with a single layer of cheese. On top of the cheese, arrange 3 rows of olives close to the middle, leaving a ½-inch space from longer sides. Sprinkle surface with pignoli and rosemary. Roll meat tightly, beginning from one of the long sides. Fasten roll about every inch, with tightly tied string.

Place pork roll into a 3-quart microwave casserole with lid. Pour wine over roast. Cook on High for 15 minutes, rotating dish once. Turn meat and baste. Re-cover and cook on *Medium* (50% power) for 50 to 60 minutes, or until a meat thermometer registers 170°F, turning meat over and basting halfway through cooking. Rotate dish 2 or 3 times throughout cooking. Allow to stand, covered, for 10 minutes before serving.

To serve: Slice between strings and untie each piece. Serve hot or chilled.

Wine Selection: Pinot Grigio or Pinot Bianco

TIP   Covering pork roast and cooking it on a lower power (Medium) for a longer period of time ensures that it will be cooked through evenly. Standing time further equalizes temperature and makes slicing easier.

SERVING SUGGESTION   Begin with Carciofi Ripieni, Stuffed Artichokes (see Index).

Costolette di Maiale alla Napoletana
NEOPOLITAN PORK CHOPS

Servings: 6   Cooking time: 20 minutes

6 pork chops, ½ inch thick
1 tablespoon olive oil
1 garlic clove, minced
½ teaspoon salt
¼ teaspoon freshly ground
   pepper
1 tablespoon chopped fresh basil,
   or ½ teaspoon crushed dried

1 green pepper, seeded and cut
   into ¼-inch squares
1 cup peeled and chopped ripe
   tomatoes, preferably plum, or
   undrained canned, chopped
Chopped fresh parsley, as
   garnish

Remove any excess outer fat from chops; freeze fat and save for sausage recipe (see Index).

In a 2-quart microwave dish (12 x 8 inches), combine oil and garlic. Cook on High for 30 to 45 seconds, until garlic is tender but not brown. Add salt, black pepper, basil, green pepper, and tomatoes; stir. Cook on High for 5 minutes, stirring halfway through cooking.

Place chops in dish with the thicker edges toward the outside. Cover with wax paper. Cook on High for 14 to 16 minutes, until chops are cooked through (no pink juices when cut next to the bone), turning over and repositioning chops halfway through cooking. Rotate dish 2 or 3 times throughout cooking. Allow to stand for 5 minutes. Spoon sauce over chops to serve.

Wine Selection: Taurasi

TIP   Wax paper holds in steam to cook chops thoroughly but allows some steam to escape to prevent sauce from becoming too watery.

SERVING SUGGESTIONS   Serve with Zucchini Ripieni, Stuffed Zucchini, or Zucchini in Insalata, Zucchini Salad (see Index for pages).

Salsiccie con Seme di Finocchi
SWEET SAUSAGE WITH FENNEL SEEDS

We include this recipe because it is not always possible to purchase good Italian sausage, and its flavor is important to any dish in which it is used. The basic recipe is a sweet fennel sausage, but there are variations for hot pepper, and cheese and parsley. We do not give directions for stuffing the sausage into casings because sausage cooks better outside of the casing in the microwave.

Quantity: about 1½ pounds   **Preparation time: 10 to 15 minutes, plus 24 hours to refrigerate**

1 pound boneless pork butt
¼ pound fresh pork fat (cut from other pork before cooking or from your butcher)
2 garlic cloves, minced
1½ teaspoons fennel seeds, crushed

1 teaspoon salt
¼ teaspoon freshly ground pepper
⅛ teaspoon crushed dried thyme

Cut meat and fat into 2-inch cubes. Using a food processor or the finest blade of a meat grinder, grind half of the meat at a time to make a coarse blend. In a mixing bowl, blend ground meat with seasonings, using a spoon or your hands (dip hands into cold water to prevent sticking).

Cover and refrigerate for 24 hours to develop flavor. Form into ½-inch-thick patties, and cook or freeze, or package sausage in bulk for future use.

VARIATIONS   For Salsiccie con Peperoncini, Sausage with Hot Peppers, add 1 to 2 teaspoons crushed red pepper.

For Salsiccie con Parmigiano e Prezzemolo, Sausage with Cheese and Parsley, add ½ cup grated Parmesan cheese and ¼ cup finely chopped fresh parsley.

Salsiccie e Peperoni
SAUSAGE AND PEPPERS

A quick family dish that is good as a stew or sandwich filling.

Servings: 4   **Cooking time: about 10 minutes**

1½ cups Salsiccie with fennel or
  hot pepper (preceding recipes),
  or packaged sausage with
  casings removed
1 cup peeled and chopped ripe
  tomatoes, preferably plum, or
  undrained canned, chopped

½ teaspoon salt
¼ teaspoon freshly ground
  pepper
3 bell peppers, seeded and cut
  into ¼-inch strips

Place a large microwave browning dish in the oven and preheat according to manufacturer's instructions for sausage, for about 6 to 8
minutes on High. Place sausage on heated dish and cook on High for
4 minutes, stirring and turning sausage over halfway through cooking.

   In a 2-quart microwave dish (12 x 8 inches) combine tomatoes,
salt, and black pepper. Cook on High for 3 minutes, stirring once halfway through cooking. Add browned sausage and bell pepper strips.
Cook on High for 6 to 7 minutes, until peppers are tender, stirring once
or twice during cooking. Allow to stand for 2 minutes.

   Serve with Italian bread or on large rolls as sandwiches.

   Wine Selection: Ciro' Rosso

TIP   Sausage is cooked before being added to tomato mixture, so
that the final mixture may be cooked until peppers are tender-crisp
or tender, depending on your preference.

9

Verdure

Vegetables

There's a slogan on the stone archway to the town of Amalfi dating back hundreds of years. It states, "When an Amalfian reaches the pearly gates, the grandeur will be just like any other day for an Amalfian."

Quite presumptuous! But when you stand at the port of Amalfi overlooking the sparkling sapphire waters of the Bay of Salerno, and tip your head back to take in the dizzying mountain heights bursting with vineyards, you can almost agree with those Amalfians.

The Almalfi coast is best known by its close proximity to the Isle of Capri, but Amalfi and the surrounding area are renowned for their quality produce, not the least of which are San Marzano tomatoes which grow in the volcanic soils near Pompeii. The temperate climate and sea air are given credit for the superb vegetables of this area.

Like every course in Italian cooking, the vegetable dish commands its own place in the meal and is never crowded together with a meat on the same plate, unless that meat is traditionally served with a vegetable. Vegetables will be served alongside the main course but on a separate plate. At a more formal meal one might want to abide by this rule, but in everyday eating we feel rules are made to be broken (if only to save washing a separate plate).

Italians prefer to cook their vegetables so that they remain firm but are soft enough to be eaten with a fork. We designed eggplant and mushroom recipes to be cooked this way. A good example of a popular Italian vegetable combination is Melanzane e Pomodori, where small eggplants are sliced while still attached to the blossom, and the slices then interspersed with fresh tomato. Garlic, basil, and onion add irresistible savor, and the presentation is showstopping. This is a vegetable mélange that deserves a course of its own.

We have still kept in mind the American penchant for tender-crisp vegetables and have cooked the Broccoli all'Olio e Aglio and Zucchini Rapido to this specification. We think you will be intrigued with the unique way we treated green onions in Cipolline in Agrodolce, Sweet and Sour Green Onions—a light and refreshing vegetable.

Salads are never served before the main course, but always afterwards to clear the palate for the meal's end. We have given a basic salad dressing that can be tossed with mixed greens, or spooned over warm cooked cauliflower, green beans, or zucchini. For an excellent winter salad, choose Cavolfiore in Insalata, a steamed head of cauliflower that is marinated in garlic-flavored oil.

Carciofi
ARTICHOKES

Servings: 4   **Cooking time: 10 to 15 minutes**

4 medium-size artichokes
Lemon juice
¼ cup water

Cut off stems and about ¾ inch of tops of the artichokes. Pull off the few tough bottom leaves and, with scissors, snip off tip of each outer leaf. Rub entire outside with lemon juice to prevent discoloration.

In a 2-quart microwave casserole, pour in water and arrange artichokes, base down. Cover with lid or vented plastic wrap and cook on High for 9½ to 14½ minutes, until lower leaves can be pulled out and the base pierces easily, rotating dish 2 to 3 times. Allow to stand, covered, for 5 minutes.

Peperoni Arrosti
ROASTED PEPPERS

The traditional Italian method of roasting peppers is to place them under the broiler until they blister or brown. We found that roasting the peppers on the microwave browning dish was a viable alternative. This is especially true when roasting smaller amounts of peppers, and it provides a welcome relief from kitchen heat in the summer when peppers are most prolific.

Quantity: 2 or 4 peppers   **Cooking time: 4 to 8 minutes**

*2 or 4 red or green sweet
    peppers*

Place microwave browning dish in oven and preheat according to manufacturer's instructions for steaks, between 4 and 8 minutes on High depending on dish size.

Meanwhile, quarter 2 peppers and remove seeds. Score the inside of the peppers so that the skin can be pressed flat against browning dish.

Place quarters from 2 peppers, skin side down, onto hot browning dish and press down with spatula. Cook on High for 4 minutes until pepper skins are browned and blistered, rotating dish and pressing peppers down again halfway through cooking.

Place heated peppers in a small brown paper bag and fold the top closed to hold in the steam. Allow to stand for 10 to 15 minutes.

If roasting more than 2 peppers, reheat the browning dish for 3 to 6 minutes until very hot. Follow the same procedure with remaining 2 peppers.

After standing time in bag is completed, place peppers under cold running water and remove charred skins.

TIPS   The peppers are quartered and scored so that more of the skin will make surface contact with the browning dish.

The browning dish can be easily cleaned to remove any dark spots left from cooking the peppers. Combine ¼ cup each of liquid Clorox and water and pour onto browning dish. Allow to stand for 2 to 6 hours, until solution becomes clear. Don't scrub, but simply rinse.

SERVING SUGGESTIONS   Use in Insalata di Riso, Rice Salad, or serve with Bagna Cauda, Anchovy Dip (see Index for pages).

Fagioli
DRIED BEANS

Dried beans are very economical, and superior in texture to canned varieties, which are softer and sometimes mushy.

If you have not soaked beans the night before, you will get the same result using the following method.

SPEED SOAKING

Beans	Water	1st Setting	2nd Setting
1 cup dried	2 cups	High for 5 to 6 min	Medium for 2 min
2 cups dried	3 cups	High for 7 to 10 min	Medium for 2 min

Cover beans with cold water in a 3- or 4-quart microwave casserole. Cover with lid or vented plastic wrap and bring to a rapid boil by setting first power level on High for time above. Stir. Set second power level on *Medium* (50% power) for 2 minutes. Let beans stand, covered, for 1 hour.

Use the following method to cook soaked dried beans:

COOKING SOAKED BEANS

Soaked Beans	Water	Yield
1 cup	2 cups	2 to 2½ cups
2 cups	3 cups	4 to 5 cups

Drain soaked beans and rinse. Place in a 3- or 4-quart microwave casserole and cover with cold water. Cover dish with lid or vented plastic wrap. Cook on High for 10 to 15 minutes, or until water boils; stir. Re-cover and cook on *Medium* (50% power) for 30 to 40 minutes, or until beans are tender. Allow to stand, covered, for 5 minutes.

Broccoli all'Olio e Aglio
BROCCOLI WITH OIL AND GARLIC

Servings: 4   Cooking time: about 8 minutes

1 bunch of fresh broccoli   2 garlic cloves, minced, or more
2 tablespoons water   to taste
2 tablespoons olive oil   ½ teaspoon salt

Cut broccoli heads into flowerets about 3 inches in length. Cut off tough ends from broccoli stems. Peel thin green skin from stems and cut stems into ½-inch rounds.

Place broccoli in a 2-quart microwave casserole with lid. Add water. Cook on High for 6 to 8 minutes, until tender-crisp, stirring once. Drain and re-cover.

In a 1-cup glass measure or custard cup combine oil and garlic. Cook on High for 45 seconds, until garlic is tender but not brown. Pour over broccoli. Add salt and toss well. Serve.

VARIATIONS   For Fagiolini all'Aglio, Green Beans with Garlic, remove stems and tips from 1 pound fresh green snap beans; cut beans into 1½-inch pieces. Increase water to ¼ cup. Cover and cook on High for 8 to 12 minutes until beans are tender-crisp, stirring once. Drain. Pour garlic oil over beans and sprinkle with salt. Toss well and serve.

Pomodori al Forno
BAKED TOMATOES

Because of their higher water content, tomatoes, mushrooms, and zucchini are generally cooked uncovered.

Servings: 4   Cooking time: 3 to 5 minutes

4 firm ripe tomatoes, each about   2 tablespoons chopped fresh
   3 inches in diameter   basil, or ½ teaspoon crushed
¼ cup fine dry bread crumbs   dried
3 tablespoons olive oil   ¼ teaspoon salt
3 tablespoons chopped parsley   Freshly ground pepper
2 tablespoons finely chopped
   onion

Remove stems from tomatoes. Cut each tomato crosswise into halves. Place tomato halves, cut side up, in a 9-inch round microwave dish.

In a small bowl, combine remaining ingredients, using pepper to taste. Spoon mixture on top of tomatoes, dividing it evenly among them. Cook on High for 3 to 5 minutes, until tomatoes are heated through, rotating dish once. Allow to stand for 1 minute before serving.

Melanzane alla Parmigiana
EGGPLANT WITH PARMESAN

Servings: 4   Cooking time: 18 to 25 minutes

2 small or 1 medium-size   ¼ cup grated Parmesan cheese
   eggplant, about 1½ pounds   2 cups Salsa di Pomodoro III
1 egg, beaten   (see Index), or prepared
2 tablespoons olive oil   tomato sauce
½ cup fine dry bread crumbs
8 ounces mozzarella cheese,
   coarsely grated

Wash eggplant and cut into ¾-inch-thick slices.

In a pie plate or shallow dish, combine egg and oil. Place bread crumbs in another shallow dish. Dip each slice of eggplant first into the egg mixture, then into the bread crumbs to coat.

Place eggplant in a single layer (overlapping slightly if necessary) in a 2-quart microwave dish (12 x 8 inches). Cook on High for 10 to 15 minutes, until tender, repositioning slices and rotating dish once or twice during cooking.

Sprinkle eggplant with 5 ounces mozzarella and 3 tablespoons Parmesan. Spoon tomato sauce over all. Sprinkle remaining 3 ounces mozzarella and 1 tablespoon Parmesan on top. Cook on *Medium* (50% power) for 8 to 10 minutes, or until cheeses are melted, rotating dish once or twice.

TIPS   Recipe is cooked uncovered to prevent sogginess.
Cooking the eggplant with the cheese is done on Medium power for more even heating and to prevent cheese from becoming rubbery.

Melanzane e Pomodori
EGGPLANT AND TOMATOES

Each serving makes an attractive fan of rosy tomatoes alternating with purple eggplants.
Servings: 4   Cooking time: about 12 minutes

2 tablespoons olive oil
1 medium-size onion, chopped
  fine
2 garlic cloves, minced
½ teaspoon salt
¼ teaspoon freshly ground
  pepper
4 small eggplants, about 4
  ounces each

3 plum or small ripe tomatoes,
  each cut into 4 slices
1 tablespoon chopped fresh basil,
  or 1 teaspoon crushed dried
2 tablespoons chopped fresh
  parsley

In a 2-quart microwave dish (12 x 8 inches) combine 1 tablespoon oil with onion and garlic. Cook on High for 1½ to 2 minutes, or until garlic and onion are slightly tender. Stir in salt and pepper.

Slice eggplants lengthwise into 4 sections, leaving the slices attached at the stem ends. Place a tomato slice between eggplant slices. Place in dish with garlic and onion. Drizzle with remaining 1 tablespoon oil and sprinkle with basil and parsley. Cover with vented plastic wrap. Cook on High for 8 to 10 minutes, until eggplants are tender, repositioning eggplants and rotating dish once. Allow to stand, covered, for 2 minutes.

To serve: Spoon some of the juices over each eggplant and place on serving plates.

Spinaci Saltati
SAUTÉED SPINACH

Servings: 4   Cooking time: about 10 minutes

2 pounds fresh spinach, or 2
  packages (about 10 ounces
  each) frozen spinach
2 tablespoons olive oil

2 garlic cloves, minced
½ teaspoon salt
⅛ teaspoon freshly ground
  pepper

Wash spinach well in 2 separate baths of water. Remove tough stems and cut larger leaves into halves.

In a 4-quart microwave casserole with lid combine oil and garlic. Cook for 30 to 45 seconds, or until garlic is tender but not brown. Add fresh or frozen spinach. Cover and cook on High for 8 to 10 minutes, until spinach is tender, stirring occasionally. Add salt and pepper; stir well.

VARIATION   For Spinaci alla Romana, Roman-Style Spinach, follow basic recipe method. Stir in 2 tablespoons each of raisins and pine nuts with salt and pepper.

TIP   Use this method for cooking other leafy vegetables like escarole or Swiss chard.

Fagiolini al Pomodoro
GREEN BEANS WITH TOMATO AND GARLIC

Servings: 4   Cooking time: 9 to 13 minutes

1 pound green snap beans   *½ teaspoon salt*
1 tablespoon olive oil   *⅛ teaspoon freshly ground*
2 garlic cloves, minced   *pepper*
1 fresh sage leaf, chopped, or ¼
*   teaspoon powdered*
½ cup peeled and chopped ripe
*   tomatoes, preferably plum, or*
*   undrained canned, chopped*

Wash beans, remove stems and tips, and cut into 1½-inch lengths. In a 2-quart microwave casserole with lid combine oil and garlic. Cook on High for 30 to 45 seconds, or until garlic is tender but not brown. Stir in sage and tomatoes. Add seasoning and beans and stir. Cover and cook on High for 8 to 12 minutes, until beans are tender-crisp, stirring halfway through cooking. Allow to stand, covered, for 2 minutes.

TIP   Tomatoes take the place of additional liquid, adding flavor and color as well.

Cipolline in Agrodolce
SWEET-AND-SOUR GREEN ONIONS

Green onions are cooked until they lose their pungent onion flavor and are very tender. We found this vegetable to be a delightful change and, because of the hint of lemon, very complementary to fish.

Servings: 4   Cooking time: 6 to 7 minutes

1 large unblemished lemon   *¼ cup chicken stock*
½ to ¾ pound (about 3 bunches)   *2 teaspoons sugar*
*   green onions*   *Salt*

Peel lemon, spiraling from top to bottom to produce one wide, long peel. Cut peel lengthwise into quarters to form 4 long thin strips. Set aside. Extract 1 teaspoon lemon juice (the rest can be refrigerated for another use).

Remove tips and ends of green onions, and peel outer layer. Divide onions into 4 bunches, tying each with a strip of lemon peel. Arrange bunches of onions in a 2-quart microwave dish (12 × 8 inches).

In a small bowl, combine 1 teaspoon lemon juice, the chicken stock, sugar, and salt to taste. Cook on High for 1 to 2 minutes, or until hot. Pour over onions.

Cover onions with plastic wrap. Cook on High for 3 minutes. Rearrange bunches from the inside to the outside. Re-cover and cook for 2 to 3 minutes more, until tender. Allow to stand for 2 minutes.

Funghi Trifolati

MUSHROOMS WITH GARLIC AND PARSLEY

Servings: 4   Cooking time: 5 minutes

1 pound fresh mushrooms
1 tablespoon butter
2 tablespoons olive oil
2 garlic cloves, chopped fine

3 tablespoons finely chopped
  fresh parsley
Freshly ground pepper

Wipe mushrooms clean and cut lengthwise into ¼-inch slices.

In a 2-quart microwave dish (12 x 8 inches), combine butter, oil, and garlic. Cook on High for 1 minute, or until garlic is tender.

Add mushrooms and stir. Cook on High for 4 to 5 minutes, or until tender, stirring once halfway through cooking. Sprinkle with parsley, and pepper to taste. Serve immediately with veal or beef, or allow to cool to room temperature for an *antipasto*.

Piselli con Prosciutto
PEAS SAUTÉED WITH PROSCIUTTO

Great flavor combination!

Servings: 4   Cooking time: 6 to 8 minutes

2 tablespoons olive oil
2 garlic cloves, minced
3 tablespoons ½-inch strips of
  thin-sliced prosciutto
2 pounds fresh garden peas,
  shelled, or 1 package (about 10
  ounces) frozen peas

2 tablespoons chopped fresh
  parsley
¼ teaspoon salt
⅛ teaspoon freshly ground
  pepper

In a 1½-quart microwave casserole with lid, combine oil, garlic, and prosciutto. Cook on High for 1 minute, until garlic is tender but not brown. Stir in peas. Cover and cook on High for 5 to 7 minutes, or until peas are tender, stirring halfway through cooking. Add parsley, salt, and pepper; stir. Serve.

Patate al Rosmarino
POTATOES WITH ROSEMARY

Servings: 4 to 6   Cooking time: about 10 minutes

1½ pounds potatoes
3 tablespoons olive oil
1 teaspoon finely chopped fresh
  rosemary, or ½ teaspoon
  crushed dried

½ teaspoon salt
¼ teaspoon freshly ground
  pepper

Peel potatoes and cut into ½-inch cubes. In a 2-quart microwave casserole with lid, combine all ingredients and stir well to coat. Cover and cook on High for 10 to 12 minutes, until tender, stirring 3 or 4 times.
    Serve immediately.

Pure di Patate
MASHED POTATOES WITH PARMESAN CHEESE

Servings: 4   Cooking time: about 10 minutes

1 pound potatoes	*⅓ cup grated Parmesan cheese*
3 tablespoons butter	*¼ teaspoon salt*
½ cup milk	*⅛ teaspoon white pepper*

Peel potatoes and cut into ¼-inch slices. In a 1½-quart microwave casserole with lid, combine potatoes, butter, and milk. Cover and cook on High for 10 to 12 minutes, or until potatoes are tender, stirring twice. Mash or beat until puréed. Stir in remaining ingredients. Serve.

TIPS   If you want creamier mashed potatoes, add 1 to 2 tablespoons more milk after mashing.
Prepare recipe in advance and Reheat (80% power) for 2 to 3 minutes.

Zucchini Rapido
QUICK ZUCCHINI

The letters *ini* on the end of an Italian word generally mean "little." Zucchini means little *zucca*, or squash.

Servings: 4   Cooking time: 3 to 5 minutes

2 medium-size zucchini	*1 tablespoon olive oil*
1 tablespoon butter	*2 garlic cloves, minced*

Wash zucchini but do not peel. Remove ends. Cut into thin matchsticks or coarsely grate.
In a 1-quart microwave casserole, combine butter, oil, and garlic. Cook on High for 30 to 45 seconds, until garlic is tender but not brown. Stir in zucchini and coat well. Cook on High for 2½ to 4 minutes until tender-crisp, stirring once. Serve.

VARIATION   For Carote e Zucchini Rapido, Quick Carrots and Zucchini, substitute 1 large carrot for 1 zucchini. Follow basic recipe instructions.

Zucchini Ripieni
STUFFED ZUCCHINI

Servings: 4   Cooking time: about 5 minutes

2 medium-size zucchini
3 tablespoons olive oil
2 garlic cloves, minced
½ cup fine dry bread crumbs
2 tablespoons grated Parmesan
  cheese

2 tablespoons chopped fresh
  parsley
¼ teaspoon chopped fresh or
  dried orégano
8 cherry tomatoes, each cut in
  half

Wash zucchini but do not peel. Cut lengthwise into halves and scoop out seeds. Place zucchini, cut side up, in a microwaveproof plate or serving platter. Set aside.

In a small microwaveproof bowl, combine 1 tablespoon oil and the garlic. Cook on High for 30 to 45 seconds, until garlic is tender but not brown. Add remaining 2 tablespoons oil and remaining ingredients except tomatoes; mix well.

Divide bread crumb mixture among 4 zucchini halves, stuffing into the hollows. Arrange 4 tomato halves on top of each. Cook on High for 3½ to 5 minutes, or until zucchini are tender-crisp, rotating once during cooking.

Salsa per Insalata
SALAD DRESSING

Before serving the dressed salad you should always taste to see if you wish to add more oil, vinegar, salt, or pepper.

Quantity: about ⅓ cup   Preparation time: 5 minutes

¼ cup olive oil
2 tablespoons wine vinegar
½ teaspoon salt

¼ teaspoon freshly ground
  pepper

Prepare salad. Add each ingredient to salad, individually, in the order listed. Toss after each ingredient is added.

Cavolfiore in Insalata
CAULIFLOWER SALAD

A winter favorite.

Servings: 6   Cooking time: about 8 minutes

1- to 1½-pound head of   Salsa per Insalata, Salad Dressing
*   cauliflower   (preceding recipe)*

Break off outer leaves and trim stem close to cauliflower head. Wash head and wrap tightly in plastic wrap. Place on a plate with the sealed edges down. Cook on High for 6 to 8 minutes, or until tender, turning head over once during cooking. Allow to stand for 3 minutes.

Meanwhile, in a medium-size bowl, combine salad dressing ingredients. Unwrap cauliflower and cut into flowerets. Add to dressing and toss. Serve at room temperature.

Zucchini in Insalata
ZUCCHINI SALAD

Servings: 4   Cooking time: about 5 minutes

1 pound zucchini, cut into ¼-   ¼ teaspoon freshly ground
*   inch slices   pepper*
¼ cup olive oil   2 tablespoons chopped fresh
2 tablespoons lemon juice   parsley
½ teaspoon salt

Place zucchini in a 1-quart microwave casserole with lid. Cover and cook on High for 4 to 5 minutes, until tender-crisp, stirring once. Allow to stand, covered, for 2 minutes.

Toss with oil, then lemon juice. Add salt, pepper, and parsley; toss. Serve at room temperature.

Fagiolini in Insalata
GREEN BEAN SALAD

Servings: 4   **Cooking time: about 10 minutes**

1 pound green snap beans
½ cup water
Salad Dressing (see Index)

Wash beans and remove stems and tips. Cut beans into halves.

Place beans in a 2-quart microwave casserole with lid. Add water. Cover and cook on High for 8 to 12 minutes, or until beans are tender-crisp, stirring once. Allow to stand, covered, for 2 minutes.

Drain and toss with dressing. Serve at room temperature.

SERVING SUGGESTIONS   Serve on a plate lined with red-tipped or Bibb lettuce or radicchio.

10
Dolci
Desserts

We will never again eat vanilla *gelato* (ice cream) without thinking of avalanches, or chocolate truffles without being reminded of an aerial café in Pizzo.

That is because dessert in Italy is more than something to cap off a meal. It is more than another course where overindulging is required and a labor of love goes unappreciated. Italian desserts bring to mind specific people, places, and incidents. For the Italians, it may be a memory of Sunday afternoons with the family and *bambini*, or of a sweltering day in Rome, assuaged only by ice cream from a sidewalk café.

But for us, the travelers, it was the sensational that we associated with Italian desserts. For it was in Livigno, a ski village just four miles from Switzerland, that we boarded the chair lift right after eating a *coppa di gelato* at a nearby lodge. As we were slowly hoisted into the cobalt blue sky, we saw a skier stumble directly below us. In an instant the snow came alive at his feet. Great, heaving, white mounds began to inch downward like a tidal wave in slow motion. Fortunately, the skier dusted himself off and schussed away unhurt. In our relief, we have turned visions of that treacherous snow into mounds of creamy gelato.

At the other end of the country, in a town called Pizzo, the search for the best chocolate dessert led a group of us to a little café that was renowned for its sweets. One *tartufo* or truffle consisted of a rich, inner core of chocolate, surrounded by a layer of chocolate and crushed nuts, all coated in powdered bittersweet chocolate. The view of the Tyrrhenian Sea from this vantage point was dizzying, but it was the chocolate that left us breathless.

This is not to say that we needed dramatics to enjoy an Italian dessert. Our only necessity was a cup of excellent Italian coffee. Late in the afternoon, or late in the evening, we might order Italian espresso with a dense almond, pignoli and chocolate cake called Torta di Mandorle e Pignoli. Midmorning coffee might dictate a lighter yellow génoise sprinkled with confectioners' sugar. (After all, the génoise was known in Genoa before it ever made its way into France). In Sicily, the layers of yellow cake are sandwiched between a ricotta cheese and candied fruit filling for a festive Cassata Ricotta. Crostata di Frutta Fresca, fresh fruit tart, is best with a cup of frothy *cappuccino*. All the desserts mentioned above are within your grasp as you follow the recipes in this chapter. You will be pleased with the effortless manner in which you can make the génoise cake, or the crispy pastry crust called for in the fruit tart.

Even with our affection for between-meal sweets, we still found that Italian desserts are the best way to celebrate the finale of a special meal. Our entertaining menus will provide you with ideas as to where they fit in best.

It was our consensus that it is almost as hard to find a bad dessert in Italy as it is bad coffee. Thus we can only suggest that you get your coffee up to snuff, for the desserts that you will be making require nothing less than the best to forge your own lasting memories.

Crema Pasticcera
PASTRY CREAM

Crema Pasticcera is a basic custard used in many desserts, but it is often tricky to make on top of the stove. Heat can be difficult to control, and constant stirring while the cream slowly thickens is tedious. This is all a thing of the past for now it takes less than 10 minutes to make the *crema* in the microwave.

Quantity: about 2 cups   **Cooking time: less than 10 minutes plus 30 to 45 minutes to cool**

1½ cups milk   4 large egg yolks, beaten
½ cup sugar   1 teaspoon vanilla, kirsch, or
¼ cup flour   rum

Pour milk into a 4-cup glass measure, and cook on High for 3 minutes; milk will be steaming but not yet boiling.

In a separate 2-quart microwave casserole, combine sugar and flour. Beat in egg yolks. Gradually add warm milk to egg mixture, beating constantly. Cook on High for 1 minute; beat. Cook for 2 to 3 minutes more, or until cream is thickened and almost ready to boil, stirring every 30 to 45 seconds. Don't allow to boil!

Remove from oven and beat in vanilla or liqueur. Cool cream, stirring occasionally to prevent a skin from forming. Mixture may be put in freezer at this point for 30 minutes to speed cooling.

TIPS   . Another way to prevent a skin from forming is to rub the top of the cream, as it begins to cool, with a little piece of butter. The butter will melt from the heat of the warm cream and coat the top.

Covered tightly, the cream can be stored in the refrigerator for 2 to 3 days.

Crostata di Frutta Fresca
FRESH FRUIT TART

This light crispy crust is patterned with a colorful carnival of fruits. It is just the right choice for rounding out a heavy meal, and an ideal focal point for a buffet table.

Servings: 6 to 8   Cooking time: 20 minutes including all recipes

1 cup flour
1 tablespoon sugar
⅛ teaspoon salt
5 tablespoons butter, cut into 20 cubes
1 egg, slightly beaten
½ cup Crema Pasticcera, Pastry Cream (see Index)
1 pint strawberries, cut into halves

15 to 20 green grapes, seeded and cut into halves
1 orange, thinly sliced, each slice cut into halves
½ cup apricot preserves
1 kiwi fruit, peeled and sliced
¼ cup blueberries

In a large mixing bowl or on a countertop, combine flour, sugar, and salt; mix well. Cut in butter with fingertips, pastry blender, or 2 knives, working quickly, until particles are pea-size.

Stir in egg with fork, and form dough into a ball. Do not overwork or dough will become tough. Flatten ball into a ½-inch rectangle approximately 5 x 4 inches; this will make dough easier to roll out later. Cover with plastic wrap and refrigerate for 1 hour, or up to 3 days.

Prepare Pastry Cream; chill.

On a lightly floured flat work surface, roll out pastry to a ⅛-inch rectangle, about 9 x 12 inches, or a size to fit your serving dish. Trim edges with a pastry cutter or sharp knife.

Place dough on top of a double sheet of wax paper. Prick top surface of pastry with a fork every ½ inch or so, and place on bottom shelf of oven. Cook on High for 5 to 7 minutes, or until pastry is almost dry, opaque, and cooked through (it will not brown), rotating 2 to 3 times. Allow to stand in oven for 5 minutes before removing. While cooling, prepare fruits.

Transfer pastry to a flat serving platter.

Spread ½ cup Pastry Cream on pastry shell, leaving ½ inch free around the edge. Reserve the remaining cream for another tart or serve with fresh fruit. Arrange strawberries around the outer edge of cream, followed by an inner row of grapes.

In a 1-cup glass measure, combine orange slices and preserves. Stir to cover orange slices. Cook on High for 1½ to 2 minutes until boiling, stirring once. With fork, gently remove orange slices and arrange a row angled against the grapes. Strain cooked preserves and reserve.

Arrange slices of kiwi fruit interspersed with blueberries on area of pastry cream that remains uncovered. With pastry brush, generously glaze entire surface of tart, fruit, and crust, with strained apricot preserves. Chill and serve.

Wine Selection: Vino Santo or Moscato d'Asti

VARIATION   Substitute ½ cup Zabaione (see Index) for Pastry Cream.

Génoise

GENOA CAKE

This light yellow cake, when unadorned, is perfect with midmorning *caffelatte* (milky coffee). But if you are the kind who thinks that a cake without icing is like a day without sun, you'll opt for the pastry cream topping in the variation.

Servings: 8   **Cooking time: about 10 minutes**

3 large eggs, beaten
⅔ cup sugar
2 ounces butter
¾ cup flour
¼ teaspoon cream of tartar

1 teaspoon baking powder
1 teaspoon grated lemon rind
2 tablespoons confectioners'
    sugar

Prepare pan by cutting a circle of wax paper to fit exactly into the bottom of a 9-inch microwave cake dish.

In a medium-size bowl, combine eggs and sugar; beat with an electric mixer until frothy, about 8 minutes.

Place butter in a custard cup or 1-cup glass measure and cook on High for 45 seconds to 1 minute, until melted; set aside. Meanwhile, in another bowl, combine flour, cream of tartar, baking powder, and lemon rind.

Fold flour mixture into egg mixture just until dry flour is no longer visible. Fold in melted butter.

Pour batter into prepared pan. Cook on Medium (50% power) for 7 minutes, then on *High* for 1 to 3 minutes, until cake springs back and a toothpick inserted into the center comes out clean, rotating dish ¼ turn every 2 minutes. Allow cake to stand on counter for 5 minutes. Turn cake out onto cooling rack to complete cooling. Peel off wax paper.

When cool, sprinkle with confectioners' sugar. Serve with tea, coffee, or sweet wine.

TIPS   Génoise is done when cake springs back. Moist areas on the top of the cake will finish cooking during standing time. To test the moist areas for cake doneness underneath, touch lightly with fingertips. The moistness that sticks to your fingers will reveal a dry cake below.

Wax paper helps to turn out cake from dish more easily.

Air holes may appear on surface, but this is just where some of the steam has escaped during cooking. When turned out, the cake will appear smooth on the surface.

VARIATION   Decorate Génoise with a pattern of vanilla and chocolate pastry creams. Prepare about 2 cups Crema Pasticcera (see Index). Measure 1 cup of warm pastry cream and set aside for the plain vanilla portion. In a microwaveproof cereal bowl, arrange 3 ounces semisweet chocolate in a circle, leaving the center free. Cook on Medium (50% power) for 1½ minutes; stir. Add 1 tablespoon butter. Cook for 1 to 1½ minutes more, or until melted, stirring every 30 seconds. Stir with the back of the spoon to smooth. Stir melted chocolate into remaining pastry cream. Cool both creams slightly.

On top of cake, lightly sprinkled with confectioners' sugar, mark out parallel rows of dots to cover the surface. Fill a pastry bag, having a medium round tip, with vanilla cream. Pipe alternating dots of vanilla cream onto marked dots on cake. Fill pastry bag with chocolate cream and fill in dots between vanilla. Whip 1 cup heavy cream with sugar to taste. Fill pastry bag, with a fluted tip, and pipe lines of cream between pastry dots and on surrounding circular edge of cake; on bottom edge, too, if desired. Chill and serve.

Cassata Ricotta
SICILIAN RICOTTA CAKE

You may find this type of cake in your favorite Italian bakery. It is a yellow génoise, lightly soaked in rum, and iced with ricotta cheese filling. A good choice for a birthday or other celebration.

Servings: 8   **Cooking time: about 10 minutes**

Génoise, Genoa Cake (preceding
  recipe)
15 ounces ricotta cheese
1 cup sugar
¼ cup light rum

1 teaspoon vanilla extract
¼ cup candied chopped fruits
¼ cup semisweet chocolate
  pieces

Split cooled cake horizontally into 3 layers.

In a large bowl, combine ricotta, sugar, 2 tablespoons rum, and the vanilla. Beat with an electric mixer until smooth. Fold in candied fruits and the chocolate pieces.

On a serving platter place one layer of the cake, cut side up. Sprinkle with 2 teaspoons rum and spread with one third of the ricotta filling. Repeat process with remaining 2 layers of cake, remaining rum and ricotta filling, using the last rum and filling on top of the cake.

Cut a piece of aluminum foil about 24 inches in length. Fold lengthwise in half and in half again. Wrap and fasten around cake to form a collar. This will keep filling in place while cake is chilling. Chill for at least 4 hours, or overnight.

Remove the foil collar from the cake. Smooth the side icing with a knife; serve.

Wine Selection: Asti Spumante

Zuppa Inglese
ITALIAN RUM CUSTARD CAKE OR "ENGLISH SOUP"

"English Soup" must have been the Italian description of the English dessert "trifle," which is alternating layers of rum-soaked cake and warm custard. The result is a concoction that resembles a creamy soup, until it is later chilled and solidified. Orange and candied fruits are added in the Italian version.

We suggest unmolding the Zuppa Inglese rather than serving it directly out of the bowl. The dome-shaped dessert makes a spectacular presentation when garnished with whipped cream and fresh strawberries.

Servings: 6   Cooking time: about 20 minutes

*Crema Pasticcera, Pastry Cream
   (see Index)*
*1 cup orange segments, chopped
   into ½-inch pieces (or other
   fruit in season)*
¼ cup candied fruits

Génoise, Genoa Cake (see Index)
5 tablespoons rum
1½ cups heavy cream
¼ cup sugar
*Strawberries, or other fruit in
   season, as garnish*

Prepare pastry cream and allow to cool. Prepare cake and allow to cool.

In a small bowl, combine 1 tablespoon rum with orange pieces and candied fruits.

Cut cake horizontally into 3 layers. Keeping layers together, cut cake into 8 wedges, from top to bottom. In a 1½-quart serving bowl, arrange one layer of cake wedges on the bottom, points to the center; sprinkle with a little rum. Spoon a little pastry cream and about 2 tablespoons fruit on top. Continue this process to fill bowl, ending with a layer of cake, sprinkled with rum. Cover dish and refrigerate overnight.

To serve: Whip cream with sugar. Loosen cake with long-bladed spatula or knife. Place serving platter on top of the bowl of cake and invert it to turn out. Fill pastry bag with whipped cream and pipe from the crown to the base of the cake to form 12 to 16 triangles. Pipe cream around the circular base of the cake. Garnish with fresh strawberries at the crown and base of cake if desired.

Torta di Mandorle e Pignoli
ALMOND AND PINE NUT CAKE

This is one of our favorites because it is satisfying but not too sweet, with its intricate blend of nuts, chocolate, Amaretto, lemon and cinnamon. The flavors are complicated but the preparation is simple. Delicious served with coffee.

Servings: 8   Cooking time: 10 minutes

9 tablespoons butter
1 cup finely ground unblanched
  almonds
¼ cup pignoli (pine nuts)
¾ cup granulated sugar
2 large eggs
2 tablespoons Amaretto, or other
  almond-flavored liqueur, or
  rum

4 ounces bittersweet chocolate,
  grated
1 cup fine dry bread crumbs
1 teaspoon baking powder
1 teaspoon grated lemon rind
¼ teaspoon ground cinnamon
Whipped heavy cream, as garnish

Coat the insides, not the bottom, of a 9-inch microwave or glass cake dish with 1 tablespoon butter. Sprinkle buttered sides with 2 tablespoons ground almonds to coat evenly. Cut round of wax paper to fit the dish, using the outside of the dish bottom to measure. Place paper in the dish and sprinkle it with pine nuts.

In a medium-size bowl, combine remaining 8 tablespoons butter with sugar, beating with electric mixer to cream mixture. In a separate bowl, stir together remaining ingredients. Add mixture to butter and sugar; mix well.

Pour batter into prepared dish. Cook on Medium (50% power) for 7 minutes, then on *High* for 1 to 3 minutes, until cake springs back and a toothpick inserted in the center comes out clean. Allow cake to stand on counter for 10 minutes. Turn cake out onto a serving dish. Peel away paper and allow cake to finish cooling.

Serve cake with whipped cream, if desired.

Wine Selection: Vino Santo

TIPS   Cake may appear slightly moist after cooking is completed. The cake will continue to cook during standing time, as long as those areas are moist and not wet. To test the moist areas for cake doneness underneath, touch those areas lightly with fingertips. The moistness that sticks to your fingers will reveal a dry cake below. A wet cake will be wet all the way through and should be cooked longer.

Zabaione
WARM WINE CUSTARD

Rich and smooth like an after-dinner drink, but better!

Servings: 4   Cooking time: about 3 minutes

4 large egg yolks   *¼ cup Marsala wine*
¼ cup sugar

Place egg yolks in a 1-quart microwave casserole and beat lightly with wire whisk. Gradually add sugar, beating with whisk to blend. Cook on Medium (50% power) for 1½ to 2 minutes, until mixture is partially cooked around the edges. Whip with whisk to incorporate air. Whisk in wine. Cook for 1 to 1½ minutes more until thickened, whipping every 30 seconds.

Remove from oven and beat with whisk for 30 seconds or so, until mixture is fluffy.

Spoon into individual stemmed glasses and serve warm.

TIP   An open bowl rather than a 4-cup measure allows for more even cooking.

If custard is overcooked, beat rapidly with an electric mixer until creamy.

VARIATION   For Zabaione Freddo, Chilled Wine Custard, prepare recipe according to basic method. After adding Marsala, pour *zabaione* into a metal bowl. Set in a larger bowl of ice cubes to cool quickly. When cooled, fold in 1 cup whipped heavy cream that is sweetened to taste. Serve over fresh fruits, or poached apples, pears, or peaches.

Pere allo Zabaione e Cioccolato
POACHED PEARS WITH WINE CUSTARD AND CHOCOLATE

An elegant winter dessert.

Servings: 4   Cooking time: about 10 minutes

4 ripe but firm pears, preferably   Zabaione Freddo (preceding
   brown Bosc   recipe)
1 lemon, cut into quarters   6 ounces semisweet chocolate
¼ cup sugar   pieces
¼ cup white wine   2 tablespoons butter, cut into 4
1 cinnamon stick   pieces

Peel each pear, leaving stems intact, and rub pears with cut lemon to prevent discoloration.

In a 1½-quart microwave casserole, combine sugar and wine; stir. Place pears on their sides in the wine, positioning them with stems toward the center. Add cinnamon stick. Cover with lid or vented plastic wrap. Cook on High for 8 to 10 minutes, or until pears are tender, turning over and basting halfway through cooking. Rotate dish twice during cooking. Baste pears and allow to cool in liquid. Meanwhile, prepare Zabaione Freddo.

Just before serving pour off pear liquid, reserving about ⅓ cup in casserole. Divide *zabaione* among 6 individual serving dishes. Stand pears, upright, on *zabaione*.

To the casserole with reserved pear liquid, add chocolate pieces. Cover and cook on High for 2 minutes, or until chocolate is melted, stirring halfway through cooking. Add butter and beat well with spoon or electric mixer until mixture is smooth. Pour over pears and serve.

TIP   Chocolate can be melted on High in this recipe, because it is combined with additional liquid. Normally chocolate is melted on Medium (50% power) to prevent overcooking and scorching.

Pesche Ripiene al Forno
BAKED STUFFED PEACHES

Servings: 4   Cooking time: about 5 minutes

2 firm ripe peaches   1 large egg yolk
¼ cup sugar   ¼ cup Amaretto or other
¼ cup chopped almonds   almond-flavored liqueur
4 amaretti cookies or almond   1 teaspoon grated lemon rind
  macaroons, crushed   4 tablespoons butter

Wash peaches and cut into halves; remove pits. Spoon out 1 tablespoon
pulp and chop fine. Place pulp in a small bowl and combine with
remaining ingredients except butter.

Divide mixture among 4 peach halves. Place 1 tablespoon of butter
on top of each. Place peach halves, filled side up, in a microwave or
glass pie plate, positioning them around the outer edge. Cover with
wax paper. Cook on High for 3 to 5 minutes until fork tender, repositioning peaches and rotating dish halfway through cooking.

Crostata di Ricotta con Amaretti
AMARETTO CHEESE PIE WITH CHOCOLATE-COVERED FRUITS

This pie combines the flavors of cheese, nuts, and fruits that are so
popular at the end of an Italian meal.

Servings: 8   Cooking time: 30 to 35 minutes

2 ounces butter   2 tablespoons Amaretto or other
¾ cup crumbs made from   almond-flavored liqueur
  amaretti or other almond-   1 teaspoon grated orange rind
  flavored cookies   16 pieces of Frutte e Noce al
½ cup finely chopped almonds   Cioccolato, Chocolate-Covered
15 ounces ricotta cheese   Fruits and Nuts (following
2 large eggs   recipe), as garnish
½ cup sugar

Place butter in a 9-inch glass or microwave pie plate. Cook on High
for 1 to 1½ minutes, or until melted. Stir in cookie crumbs and chopped

almonds until well blended. Press firmly against the bottom and sides of the dish to form a crust. Cook on High for 1½ to 2½ minutes, until set, rotating dish once.

In a medium-size mixing bowl, combine ricotta, eggs, sugar, liqueur, and orange rind. Pour into prepared pie shell. Cook on *Medium* (50% power) for 25 to 30 minutes, until center is almost set and a knife inserted 1 inch from the center comes out clean. Rotate dish ¼ turn every 5 minutes. Cool and refrigerate overnight, or for at least 8 hours.

Before serving, garnish with chocolate-covered nuts or fruits.

TIPS   If amaretti cookies are not available, substitute zwieback toast crumbs mixed with ½ teaspoon almond flavoring. Increase butter to 5 tablespoons, because zwieback crumbs are drier.

Orange rind can be grated in larger quantities than needed and frozen for later use.

The cheese pie is cooked on Medium for more even cooking.

Frutte e Noce al Cioccolato
CHOCOLATE-COVERED FRUITS AND NUTS

Quantity: about 14 pieces   **Cooking time: about 3 minutes**

6 ounces semisweet chocolate
  pieces
14 pieces of fruits or nuts, such
  as strawberries with hulls,
  orange segments, cherries,
  grapes, or almonds

Arrange chocolate pieces in a circle in a microwaveproof cereal bowl, leaving the center free. Cook on Medium (50% power) for 2 minutes; stir. Continue to cook for 1 to 1½ minutes more, until just melted, stirring every 30 seconds. Smooth with the back of a spoon.

Dip each fruit or nut into chocolate, just halfway. Place each on wax paper to cool until chocolate is set. Serve as a sweet with coffee or as a garnish for Crostata di Ricotta con Amaretti (preceding recipe).

TIP   Be sure to use real chocolate because imitation chocolate does not melt as well in the microwave.

Spuma di Bianca
WHITE CHOCOLATE MOUSSE

A quick and impressive dessert that is a pleasing alternative to dark chocolate mousse.

Servings: 6   **Cooking time: 3 minutes**

7 ounces white chocolate   1 cup heavy cream, whipped
2 tablespoons sugar   3 tablespoons rum
3 whole eggs

Coarsely chop 1 ounce chocolate; set aside.

Arrange remaining 6 ounces chocolate in a circle in a medium-size microwaveproof bowl, leaving the center free. Cook on Medium (50% power) for 2 minutes; stir. Continue to cook for 1 to 1½ minutes more, until just melted, stirring every 30 seconds. Smooth with the back of a spoon.

In another bowl, beat sugar and eggs until foamy. Stir egg mixture into chocolate, a little at a time, beating constantly with a wire whisk.

Fold in whipped cream, then the chopped 1 ounce chocolate. Spoon into individual glasses and refrigerate overnight. Serve with crisp cookies or Croccante (see Index).

VARIATION   For Spuma di Cioccolata, Chocolate Mousse, substitute 6 ounces semisweet chocolate pieces for 7 ounces white chocolate. Eliminate the extra 1 ounce coarsely chopped chocolate.

Baci di Amori
CHOCOLATE TRUFFLES OR "KISSES OF LOVE"

Baci (pronounced botchy) di Amori are the type of chocolate kisses you would pick up in a specialty store for your Valentine. Now you can prepare them yourself and they are just out of this world! Make up an assortment of all the variations as a tempting dessert tray for a buffet or brunch.

One of our favorites is the Sambuca variation, which is a licorice-flavored chocolate mixture wrapped around coffee beans. These are excellent with espresso or after-dinner drinks.

Servings: 12 to 24   **Cooking time: about 3 minutes**

6 ounces semisweet chocolate
  pieces
3 tablespoons butter
2 large egg yolks
2 tablespoons Frangelica,
  hazelnut-flavored liqueur, or
  rum

¼ cup unsweetened cocoa
  powder
2 tablespoons sifted
  confectioners' sugar
12 to 24 whole hazelnuts

Arrange chocolate pieces in a circle in a microwaveproof cereal bowl, leaving the center free. Cook on Medium (50% power) for 2 minutes; stir. Continue to cook for 1 to 1½ minutes more, until chocolate is just melted, stirring every 30 seconds. Smooth with the back of a spoon.

Soften butter to room temperature by heating on Warm (10% power) for 30 seconds. In a medium-size mixing bowl, combine softened butter, egg yolks, and liqueur. Add chocolate and beat with electric mixer until well blended. Chill for 15 minutes, until mixture can be rolled into a ball.

Meanwhile, in a small bowl or on wax paper, combine cocoa powder and confectioners' sugar.

Take between 1 and 2 tablespoons of chilled chocolate mixture depending on size desired, and roll around a hazelnut. Roll in cocoa and sugar. Chill.

Serve with espresso coffee or use as a cake garnish.

TIPS   Use real chocolate bits, not imitation, for more even melting. The better the grade of cocoa used, the richer the *baci*.

VARIATIONS   For Baci di Amori con Sambuca, Truffles with Sambuca, substitute Sambuca for rum, and coffee beans for hazelnuts. Proceed with basic recipe.

For Fichi Ripieni, Stuffed Dried Figs, follow basic recipe method until chocolate mixture is chilled. Combine cocoa and confectioners' sugar. Eliminate hazelnuts, and substitute 24 dried figs. Slit figs and insert 1 teaspoon chilled chocolate mixture into each.

Arrange 6 ounces semisweet chocolate pieces in a circle in a microwaveproof cereal bowl, leaving the center free. Cook on Medium (50% power) for 2 to 3 minutes, until melted, stirring often. Stir melted chocolate until smooth. Dip half of each stuffed fig into melted chocolate and allow to cool on wax paper until set.

Croccante
CARAMELIZED ALMOND BRITTLE

This versatile recipe can be served alone as a candy, or as an accompaniment to White Chocolate Mousse. When crushed it makes a delicious topping for vanilla or Amaretto ice cream.

Quantity: about 2½ cups   **Cooking time: about 8 minutes**

1 cup sugar   *1½ cups blanched almonds,*
½ cup white corn syrup   *coarsely chopped*

In a 1½-quart microwave casserole, combine sugar and corn syrup. Cook on High for 4 minutes. Stir in nuts and cook for 3 to 5 minutes more, or until syrup is golden in color.

Pour onto a lightly greased cookie sheet and spread to about ⅛-inch thickness. Before brittle cools completely, cut into diamond shapes. Store in a dry place.

To use as an ice cream topping, coarsely chop in blender or food processor.

Gelato di Crema
VANILLA ICE CREAM

Italians are world famous for their ice cream. Were there a shortage of their *gelati*, it would probably cause a country-wide *sciopero* (strike). It is *that* good, and they are *that* passionate about it.

What makes Italian ice cream so rich and delicious? Unlike American ice cream, it begins with a pastry cream base. After this base is cooked, heavy cream is added and the mixture is chilled. We were particularly fond of the hazelnut ice cream we found in a Roman café and hope you will try it here.

Quantity: about 1 quart   **Cooking time: about 10 minutes**

2 cups milk   *1 cup heavy cream, chilled*
1 cup sugar   *1 teaspoon vanilla extract*
4 large egg yolks   *Oil*

In a 4-cup glass measure, combine milk and ½ cup sugar. Cook on High for 3 to 5 minutes, until sugar is dissolved and milk is hot but not quite boiling, stirring once.

Meanwhile, in a medium-size bowl, beat egg yolks and remaining ½ cup sugar with a whisk until well blended. Slowly pour in ½ cup of the warm milk mixture, stirring constantly. Pour this back into the rest of the milk and sugar; beat well. Cook on *Medium* (50% power) for 4 to 5 minutes, until mixture thickens slightly and coats the back of a spoon, stirring once. Do not boil.

Stir in heavy cream and vanilla. Refrigerate for at least 1 hour.

Meanwhile, lightly oil a 6-cup loaf pan and line with plastic wrap, leaving 2 inches of wrap hanging over each side to fold back later. Set aside.

Ice cream maker method:

Pour chilled cream mixture into an ice cream maker and freeze according to manufacturer's instructions. Pour ice cream into prepared pan and smooth with a spatula. Cover with plastic wrap and foil. Freeze until ready to serve.

Freezer tray method:

Pour chilled cream mixture into a shallow metal pan or ice-cube trays with dividers removed. Freeze, stirring every 30 minutes for about 4 hours, until frozen. Process in food processor or beat with an electric mixer until mushy. Pour into a prepared loaf pan. Cover with plastic and foil until ready to serve.

To serve: Scoop ice cream into individual bowls, or unmold loaf pan onto a serving tray. Allow to soften slightly, then slice for servings.

Spoon over fresh fruits or sprinkle with powdered Croccante (see Index) and with 1 tablespoon of fruit or nut-flavored liqueur over each serving.

VARIATIONS   For Gelato di Amaretto, Amaretto Ice Cream, follow basic recipe method. When cream mixture is partially frozen in ice cream maker or freezer trays, stir in 2 tablespoons Amaretto or other almond-flavored liqueur, and 1 cup crushed Croccante (see Index).

For Gelato di Nocciuole, Hazelnut Ice Cream, follow basic recipe method. When cream mixture is partially frozen in ice cream maker or freezer trays, stir in 2 tablespoons Frangelica or other hazelnut-flavored liqueur, and 1 cup finely chopped hazelnuts.

Granita di Limone
LEMON ICE

This refreshing Italian ice is suitable as a palate cleanser between courses or a delightful dessert after a heavy meal. It is a crowd pleaser, especially when served in chilled lemon shells.

Quantity: 1 quart   **Cooking time: about 10 minutes**

2 cups sugar
3 cups water
½ cup fresh lemon juice (see
   serving suggestions below)
1 tablespoon grated lemon rind
About 12 uniform lemons as
   serving containers (optional)

In a 3-quart microwave casserole, combine sugar and water. Cook on High for 8 to 12 minutes, until sugar has dissolved, stirring once or twice. Allow to stand for 10 minutes.

Add lemon juice and rind. Pour mixture into refrigerator trays, with dividers, and chill in freezer until it is mushy. Transfer mixture to a chilled bowl or food processor bowl. Beat with electric mixer or fork, or use a processor to break up ice crystals. Return to refrigerator tray and freeze until firm but not solid.

To serve in lemon shells: While lemon ice is freezing, cut a thin slice from the bottom of each lemon (to steady on a plate for serving). Cut one third from the top and scoop out lemon pulp. You may squeeze pulp for lemon juice, freezing extra for later use. Clean inside of lemon shells with a spoon. Freeze shells for 30 minutes or so. Spoon almost frozen lemon ice into shells, packing and mounding ice into each. Re-freeze and serve with candied violets.

If not serving the ice in lemons, before it is completely frozen, spoon it into refrigerator trays or a loaf pan lined with plastic wrap. Cover with foil and re-freeze. To serve: Scoop out into sherbet glasses, or unmold loaf pan onto a serving tray.

Suggested Menus
for Entertaining

Amalfi Coast Dinner

Carciofi Ripieni   or   *Vongole Ripieni*
Stuffed Artichokes   Stuffed Clams

Spaghetti all'Aglio e Olio
Spaghetti with Garlic and Oil

Wine Selection:
Greco di Tufo

Pesce alla Senape
Fish Fillets with Mustard Mayonnaise

Wine Selection:
Verdicchio dei Castelli Di Jesi

Cipolline in Agrodolce
Sweet and Sour Green Onions

Crostata di Ricotta con Amaretti
Amaretto Cheese Pie with Chocolate-Covered Fruits

145

Summer Buffet

Pomodori con Prosciutto e Basilico
Tomatoes with Prosciutto and Basil

or

Peperoni Arrosti e Funghi all'Olio
Roasted Pepper and Mushroom Salad

Arrosto di Maiale di Capodimonte
Chilled Stuffed Rolled Pork Roast of Capodimonte

Wine Selection:
Pinot Grigio or
Pinot Bianco

Insalata
Salad

Gelato di Amaretto con Croccante
Amaretto Ice Cream with Caramelized Almond Brittle

Late Summer Meal

Caponata
Cold Eggplant Appetizer

Gnocchi di Patate con Salsa di Burro
Small Potato Dumplings with Butter Sauce

Branzino Marechiare
Sea Bass Cooked with Clams in Tomato Sauce

Wine Selection:
Trebbiano d'Abruzzo

Spuma di Bianca
White Chocolate Mousse

Winter Menu for Company

Gamberetti all'Olio e Limone
Shrimps Marinated in Oil and Lemon

Ossobuco
Veal Shanks Simmered in Sauce

Wine Selection:
Barbera

Risotto alla Milanese
Italian Rice with Saffron

Pere allo Zabaione e Cioccolato
Poached Pears with Wine Custard and Chocolate

Birthday Celebration

Cozze al Maionese con Acciuga e Capperi
Mussels with Anchovy Caper Mayonnaise

Spaghetti con Salsa dell'Olive
Spaghetti with Olive Sauce

Petti di Pollo alla Parmigiana
Breaded Chicken Cutlets with Cheese and Tomato Sauce

Wine Selection:
Greco di Tufo

Insalata
Salad

Cassata Ricotta
Sicilian Ricotta Cake

Gala Buffet

Verduri Marinati
Marinated Vegetables
and
Caprino Marinati con
Rosmarino
Goat's Milk Cheese Marinated
with Rosemary

Branzino in Bianco con Salsa Verde
Chilled Poached Bass in White
Wine with Green Sauce

Vitello Tonnato
Cold Roast Veal in Tuna
Sauce

Wine Selection:
Gavi or Vernaccia di San Gimignano

Crostata di Frutta Fresca
Fresh Fruit Tart

Granita di Limone
Lemon Ice

Baci di Amori con Sambuca
Chocolate Truffles with Sambuca

Wine Selection:
Spumante Brut

Informal Dinner

Fettuccine alla Carbonara
Fettuccine with Cream Sauce
and Bacon
or
Fettuccine alla Gorgonzola
Fettuccine with Gorgonzola
Sauce

Petti di Pollo alla Marsala
Breaded Chicken Cutlets with Marsala

Wine Selection:
Cabernet, Grave del Friuli or Collio

Melanzane e Pomodori
Eggplant and Tomatoes

Pesche Ripiene al Forno
Baked Stuffed Peaches

Index